HOW TO GAIN THE
COMPETITIVE ADVANTAGE IN SALES

COLLABORATIVE
SELLING

by RICK BARRERA, C.S.P.
& DR. TONY ALESSANDRA

Morgan James Publishing • New York

THE COMPETITIVE ADVANTAGE

ISBN: 1-933596-44-9 (Paperback)

Published by:

MORGAN · JAMES
THE ENTREPRENEURIAL PUBLISHER
www.morganjamespublishing.com

Morgan James Publishing, LLC
1225 Franklin Ave Ste 325
Garden City, NY 11530-1693
Toll Free 800-485-4943

Habitat
for Humanity®
Peninsula
Building Partner

Cover and Interior Design by:
Michelle Radomski
One to One Creative Services
www.creativeones.net

DEDICATION

▼

To Holli Olson Catchpole
Who is the epitome of a collaborative salesperson
—T.A.

To my wife and lifelong love, Keely
—R.B.

ACKNOWLEDGEMENTS

▼

We would like to thank the people without whom this book would not have been possible. Thanks to Joyce Wycoff for adding her input, insights and polish to the manuscript; to Cindy Spring for refining the script for the audio program, **The Edge,** *released by Dartnell, on which this book is based; and to the following individuals whose assistance in developing the concept for the video training series,* **The Competitive Advantage,** *contributed greatly to this work. Thank you to Sue Alessandra, Gary Alessandra, Gregg Baron, Doug Breekner, Holli Catchpole, Mike Davis, Curt Ittner, Dee Jones, Adelina Liwag, Keely Smith, Rob Sommer, and Peter Wheeler.*

RICK BARRERA
RECENT RAVE REVIEWS

▼

"You made a great case for change and differentiation, your direct approach was exactly what we needed. Your humor added fun to a serious speech and topic."

—Rentway, Inc.

"Rick knew his audience and kept them engaged... It's a great speaker who can make an audience look at themselves and start the wheels of change spinning, even when the change could be uncomfortable."

—AAA

"You provided a very 'Fast and Furious' way of energizing our team to drive innovation in a commodity based business with low margins."

—Sodexho USA

"I sat through dozens of presentations over the past 30 years and Rick was one of the most refreshing and informative presenters I have ever listened to. He gave you a lot of take away to help you improve your business."

—Notifier

"Rick did a great job in helping our group find its way toward a very aggressive business plan that we're excited about implementing. It was hard-hitting time well spent."

—Aegis Mortgage Corporation

"Delegates continue to rank him among our best speakers to date—his blend of content, delivery, and motivation is among the best we have seen. Rick's unique perspective makes a lasting impact."

—National Association of Professional Employment Organizations

"In all my years doing this, you were absolutely the very best at knowing your audience. I was so impressed with the time you took to learn about our organization. It was very obvious to our participants that his was not a 'canned' presentation, but was designed specifically to meet our needs. You were a pleasure to work with. I look forward to future opportunities."

—American Express Financial Advisors

"Rick really opened my eyes. He knew more about my business than I did."

—Lexus

"Never have I seen a speaker who knows his audience more. Unbelievable... I would recommend Rick in a heartbeat."

—Wells Fargo Merchant Services

DR. TONY ALESSANDRA'S
RECENT RAVE REVIEWS

▼

"A perfect way to end the day. Took everything learned during the day and summed it all up. Great speaker. Excellent. Upbeat!!"
—Chase Manhattan Bank

"A standing ovation and a ballroom that had more people at the end than at the beginning is a winning keynote! Your ability to relate so much of the Platinum Rule to the SUBWAY experience drove your message right to the franchisees' front doors!"
—Subway

"His enthusiasm and energy was contagious! He is an outstanding professional —we were all impressed."
—Ricoh Corporation

"Your energy, warmth, humor and command of material earned the greatest praise I've ever had for selecting and presenting a speaker. I would whole heartedly endorse you for any meeting and look forward to working with you again."
—Better Business Bureau

"As a lawyer, I'm always skeptical about great promises since expectations thus created so seldom match perceived reality. Your performance disproved my skepticism. A constant refrain in feedback was 'terrific', 'bring the fellow back', 'superb', 'thoughtful and witty'."
—Lucent Technologies

"Thank you for your terrific presentation at Countrywide's Senior Management Conference. It had a big impact on people at Countrywide. In fact, the week afterward Ojai, you couldn't walk into a meeting without hearing people analyzing each other as Thinkers, Socializers, Relaters or Directors."
—Countrywide

"Well, you did it again! Another outstanding presentation impressing a room packed with sales professionals."
—San Diego ConVis

"Our delegates were super-impressed with you and both of your presentations. They are still experiencing the afterglow!"
—National Tour Association

"He had been the unanimous choice going in and the standing ovation certainly attested to the fact that he was the right choice for our group."
—First Union Bank

"Having Tony as our first speaker set the tone for our entire meeting."

—*Kemper National Insurance*

"Your presentation at our meeting was a 'Home Run'. The Distributors couldn't stop talking about how important your message was to them. You truly 'exceeded expectations'..."

—*Toshiba*

"[I have] become an 'apostle' of Tony."

—*Caterpillar*

"Tony was terrific! My staff swears he's the best ever!"

—*Bridal Marketing Association of America*

"I've heard Tony speak three times and I enjoy him more each time. He's humorous, insightful and interesting!"

—*Allied Van Lines*

"Actionable, quick, stimulating and fun. Nobody has combined content and delivery to so excite our folks as did Tony Alessandra."

—*McGraw-Hill CIG*

"We needed someone to deliver on a closing motivational speech and Tony exceeded our expectations to a standing ovation."

—*Parke-Davis*

"Aside from exceeding our expectations, Tony did an extraordinary job in understanding our business, operations, nomenclature, culture, etc.; in a very short period of time... this truly customized his presentation to us."

—*Aramark*

"Tony was able to capture the audience attention during the first ten seconds and kept everyone involved for the full hour and a half. What a great presenter!"

—*Fetzer Vineyards*

"Thank you for your wonderful presentation... Your knowledge, charisma and professionalism were clearly evident."

—*Robert W. Baird & Co.*

"The group is still talking about your presentation..."

—*The New York Times*

"Many of our Distributors stopped me during the conference to let me know how much they appreciated the ideas you shared—ideas they could use in their business and their personal lives."

—*Tupperware*

"'Dr. Alessandra really did his homework.'"

—*Service Merchandise Company*

"Great presentation and message! Tony is outstanding. He achieved total audience participation, everyone learned while having fun. A home run."

—*Lucent Technologies*

THE COMPETITIVE ADVANTAGE
TABLE OF CONTENTS

▼

INTRODUCTION

▼

Welcome to *The Competitive Advantage,* a new kind of sales training book, designed to help you reach exceptional levels of success in today's new sales environment. The world has changed in significant ways and salespeople today are required to have new skills, new attitudes and a new understanding of how to work with their clients.

Here are a few questions that might help demonstrate this point. Have you found that your competitors are more *aggressive* than they used to be? Do you have *more* competitors than you've had in the past? Does it seem that it's harder to *sell* your product now than just a few years ago? Are you finding it harder to *differentiate* yourself from your competitors? Are *price issues* a constant problem?

If you answered "yes" to more than one of these questions, it's because your company is participating in a worldwide quantum shift that's particularly acute in the United States. There are three key aspects to this shift:

- **Technology**—for most products, **technology** is no longer a **differentia-tor.** Most of your competitors have about the same technology as you do, which means your products have about the same features. In the past, it was possible to have a technical breakthrough that would give you years of competitive advantage. Only a few companies can claim today that their product is radically different from the competition... and that difference generally lasts only a few years at most.
- **Global Market**—we're selling in a **global** marketplace, which means we have more competitors and different competitors than we've had in the past. The arrival of new competitors has also created more confusion in the marketplace... not only for us but for our customers.

- **Supply Exceeds Demand**—for most products and services, **supply exceeds demand**. In other words, there are more products and services available than the market, as a whole, wants to buy. In the past, businesses with quality products were reasonably sure they would be able to sell them. Today, that may no longer be true. Do you remember the "good old days" of 1983 when the phone company was still a monopoly and connecting new service could take weeks? Today, you have literally hundreds of choices and it takes only minutes to connect you!

What this all means is that buyers today are overwhelmed with more choices of products and suppliers than they could possibly ever use. If you want to be successful in today's market you must be able to get the buyers attention, and to do that you must be able to **differentiate** yourself, your company and your product. When the product, or the technology, or the company is not the differentiating factor, that leaves one possibility—**You.**

In the 80s you had to do more with less. Today you have to do more with less *and* do it faster. Quality that you can document is essential to survive in today's market, and exceptional customer service delivered by your company... and *you*... is more important than ever.

Today's customers aren't looking for quick fixes, either. They're looking for long-term relationships with suppliers who'll be resources for them over the long haul. Your ability to collaborate and partner with your customers will make or break your career. Your sales success in the information age will depend on your ability to learn about and adapt to the realities of a new and very different marketplace.

Another reason the selling systems of the past won't work today because they were designed to work in a different environment... an adversarial environment. Today, many companies are awarding lifetime contracts to their supplier-partners. Companies network their computer systems together for order entry, just-in-time inventory control, and electronic payment. When your customers are your partners—and you want them as **lifetime** partners—you can't sell using commando tactics. An adversarial relationship just won't work.

Selling effectively today means handling all the interpersonal aspects of a sale better than you have in the past and that's what this book is designed to help you do. We'll show you how to excel in this tougher, faster, more complex selling arena. When you really understand the tools and information in this book, you'll find that you'll win more sales, do it in less time and build a strong base of lifetime customers who will act as both references *and* sources of referrals. We'll show you how to identify your target accounts, how to sell to them without manipulation and how to penetrate each account to maximize its potential.

Whether you're a newcomer or a seasoned professional, you'll find ideas in this book that will take your selling *skills and your sales* to new levels. As you put these ideas into practice, you'll see your success with customers soar right along with your commissions. As these skills become second nature, you'll soon see yourself as a cutting edge sales professional who knows what it takes to win in the information age. In a short time you'll find that you truly do have... *The Competitive Advantage.*

What's Wrong with Traditional Selling

Throughout this book we'll be discussing the differences between our collaborative approach to selling and the traditional approach to selling. Let us explain what we mean when we use the term "traditional selling." The traditional approach to selling was largely developed during the years following World War II. When the war ended, demand for consumer goods was at an all time high and consumers were not as sophisticated as they are today. Selling involved razzle-dazzle pitches that highlighted the new technical features of the product followed by a strong close that would let the buyer know that this was their last chance to buy the product or it would be offered to someone else. The traditional salesperson needed the ability to overcome all of the buyer's objections immediately because he had to move on to the next prospect. It was strictly a one shot deal.

Today's customers buy differently. They know there's no real urgency because the good deal will still be there tomorrow or a better one may replace it. Today's customers have learned to shop around, and they know they have lots of very similar options from other vendors. They're looking for measurable quality in what they buy and for a company and a salesperson who will be there when they need help. In other words, they're not just looking to buy a product; they're looking for a long-term relationship with their supplier. Terms like strategic alliance, sustaining resource, single source, integrity, values, and ethics are increasingly being used to describe the current nature of the buyer/seller relationship. You need only look at the "green revolution" to see that the customers of today look at much more than just the product.

The traditional salesperson paid very little attention to targeting specific markets and planning their calls. Their plan was to deliver the same pitch with little variation to as many people as they could, in the shortest amount of time. When they contacted a prospect, they spent a few minutes engaging in small talk to break the ice, asked a few fact-finding questions, then launched right into their presentation with very little knowledge of the customers true needs. Their pitch had to cover all of the product's features and benefits because they couldn't be sure which ones would be relevant to their prospect. Then came the close. What do you think happened?

Let's review this by putting you in the role of the customer. A salesperson contacts you, asks you a couple of questions, delivers a presentation on a product that may have little to do with your needs and then asks you how many you'd like to buy? If you were an intelligent, reasonably assertive person, what would you say? "No!" Of course! But the salesperson expected that. Everyone says no at first! So he asks you, "Why not?" and the objection game begins. Can you think up more objections than he can overcome? If so, you win! If not, you lose! Now, think about that process: hard sales pitch unrelated to customer needs... manipulative closing tactics... high pressure attempts to overcome objections... and if you buy, the salesperson is gone... on to the next target! Is this the basis for a long-term relationship?

How many referrals would you be willing to provide after an adversarial sales process like that? How willing would you be to repeat the process in the future? And if you have a problem with the product, what would your attitude be? Would you be committed to making the product work out or just be looking for flaws? And how much follow up would you expect from this salesperson? None probably... unless he wants to sell you something else!

What's missing in traditional selling is the salesperson's commitment to a long-term relationship. Short-term thinking creates an adversarial environment and in an adversarial environment everyone loses. This whole process creates negative tension for both the buyer and the seller. Neither one is comfortable, but successful, traditional salespeople learn to live with the tension and customers learn how to avoid getting into these situations in the first place. If you want to see traditional selling in its classic form, just go to your local car dealer. Most haven't changed their sales process since the fifties. They still think short-term and they can't understand why people are avoiding buying a new car!

In a long-term relationship, you're more concerned about quality than your customers are because it supports **their** customers' purchases that in turn affects their future orders from you. Your customers are more concerned with your profitability because they want you to be a viable source of supply when it comes time to reorder.

Why Collaborative Selling Works Better

It doesn't take a genius to figure out that the emphasis in traditional selling is in the wrong place. The collaborative salesperson takes the time up-front to build a sincere, committed relationship and to learn in-depth about the customers needs. This makes the entire sales process a positive experience and it ensures that the environment will be cooperative rather than adversarial. There are six key words that describe how the collaborative sales process unfolds: *Targeting, Contacting, Exploring, Collaborating, Confirming, and Assuring.* Let's take an overview of the process:

- Target—this step helps you understand exactly what you have to offer that's unique and exactly which **target** audiences can best use what you have to sell. It takes some time, but your success ratios will be much higher because you'll be focusing your efforts only on those prospects who have a high probability of buying. Then you'll work to see that these prospects have a positive image of you *before* you call on them.

- Contact—When you do contact them you'll be prepared to convey your **advantages**, your **credibility** and your **sincere desire** to be of service. You'll develop trust and you'll gather a complete picture of their situation, their needs and their opportunities before you talk at all about your product or service. You'll let your prospect know you're there to help more than you're there to sell.

- Explore—Rather than delivering a pitch, you'll explore options with your client to develop solutions that you feel might work in his situation.

- Collaborate—Together you'll select the options that look like the best fit. Your client will have as much or more input into the creation and the selection of options as you do. This process ensures that they will be as committed to implementing the solution as you are.

After all, why would they invest their time in creating a solution they're not committed to buy?

- **Confirm**—This step is the logical conclusion to the continual communication and problem solving process you've been in with your client. You're not ending the process; you're beginning it. Confirmation becomes a question of when, not if. If resistance does occur, it simply indicates a need to gather more information or clarify some details. When your prospect has helped co-design the solution and "buys in," then you don't need to "close" him. If he feels his needs are being met, he'll buy!

- **Assure**—The final step begins immediately after the sale. You change hats from "salesperson" to "quality control person." You'll help your customers track their results and analyze the effectiveness of your solution. By assuring their satisfaction, you'll build a large, loyal clientele that will guarantee future sales and referrals.

Sounds pretty good doesn't it? If you're like most of salespeople, you're probably saying, "I sell like that already. I'm not a traditional salesperson." That's great! It probably means that you lean more toward collaborative than traditional, but you may still have some traditional tools in your sales kit. You're most likely doing what we call quasi-traditional selling. Quasi-traditional selling is where you embrace the *philosophy* of collaborative selling, but you continue to use some of the skills and techniques of traditional selling. If you still have negative tension in the sales process, or find yourself in an adversarial environment, or close hard to get the sale, or have a lot of price resistance, or find yourself handling a lot of objections, there's still some quasi-traditional selling going on.

If you're still not sure whether you may be practicing quasi-traditional selling try this quick quiz:

1. When there's a problem, do you find yourself protecting your company or your customer?
2. Do you think in terms of orders or relationships?
3. Do you try to negotiate for top dollar or look out for both best long-term interests of your customer?
4. Do you generally get one order per customer or do you fully leverage your sales activities through referrals and expansion within the customer's environment?

5. Do you make the sale and move on or measure outcomes and assure satisfaction?
6. Do you try to win vs. trying to help?
7. Do you make presentations or do you involve and facilitate?
8. Do you try to impose solutions or elicit solutions?
9. Do you avoid or ignore issues or do you work to solve issues?
10. Do you see yourself as a supplier or as an integrated partner?

If you selected the first option in any of the preceding questions you're practicing quasi-traditional selling. You may be embracing the philosophy of collaborative selling but from your client's viewpoint, it still looks like traditional selling.

Throughout this book, you'll be learning all of the specific skills and techniques you'll need to effectively practice collaborative selling, so your clients will see you as a partner rather than an adversary. This will enable you to become even more of a superstar than you are now and you'll find that selling will be even more fun as you put these techniques into practice.

If you're new to the sales profession, you'll be learning the correct way to sell right from the beginning. If you're an old pro, you'll have an opportunity to refine your skills, be reminded of some things you may have forgotten, and learn some new skills along the way.

So, let's explore together *The Competitive Advantage*... a new kind of sales training book. As you listen, picture yourself applying these ideas, hear yourself saying the words that explore, collaborate, confirm, and assure your client. Feel yourself being a friend, a partner to that person, not an adversary. Remember that the emphasis here is not so much on what you sell, but who you are in the selling situation.

STEP I

TARGETING

▼

The Targeting step of sales includes three phases: understanding and being able to state your competitive advantage; identifying and finding your best prospects; and using personal marketing techniques to generate leads.

Targeting helps you understand exactly what you have to offer that's unique and exactly which target audiences can best use what you have to sell. Until you understand what makes your product or service different from the competition, you really don't know what benefits you have to offer your customer. And, until you can state your competitive advantage in a short, simple statement, your prospects will not understand what you have to offer.

Once you understand your competitive advantage, it is important to identify the prospects who will have the highest need for your product or service. These are your best prospects... the ones who are most likely to buy, use and recommend you and your services.

When you have identified your best prospects and know where to find them, you can use your personal marketing skills to generate leads that will lead to sales. These techniques can actually help you create an environment where your prospects call you! Lead generation is the fuel that drives the engine of your sales success. The techniques discussed in this chapter can keep you in highly qualified leads for the remainder of your sales career.

Targeting takes some time, but your success ratios will be much higher because you'll be focusing your efforts only on those prospects who have a high probability of buying. Then you'll work to see that these prospects have a positive image of you *before* you call on them. When you do call them, you be able to quickly give them a powerful statement of your competitive advantage.

CHAPTER 1

YOUR COMPETITIVE ADVANTAGE

▼

As we've traveled around the country over the past several years working with salespeople we've been amazed to find that they do not know, and cannot articulate their competitive advantage! How can a salesperson expect prospects and customers to give their time and attention if they do not understand, clearly and concisely, what that salesperson can do for them that no one else can do? That's what we call selling in the pit.

Salespeople who don't understand their competitive advantage are all in a deep pit saying things like "Our product is better quality" or "Our service is better" or "I'm my company's competitive advantage." Even if a salesperson is his company's competitive advantage, he won't convince his customers just by saying so because many of his competitors will be saying the exact same thing! That's selling in the pit! To get out of the pit, the salesperson has to *define* quality. He has to *show* the prospect what outstanding service looks like and *how his service differs from the competition.*

In a moment we'll show you how to determine your competitive advantage but first let's talk about how you can demonstrate your competitive advantage from the very first moment you are introduced. Suppose someone walks up to you at a business conference, introduces herself, and asks you what you do for a living. *Exactly* what would you say?

Did you have any trouble? Did you stumble? Do you know what sets you apart from your competitors? If this was hard for you, you're not alone. If you were to ask the average car, computer or caviar salesperson what they do for a living they'll probably say, "I sell cars, computers or caviar." But what does every other car, computer or caviar salesperson say?... Exactly the same thing!

So what *should* the salesperson who understands his competitive advantage say? How about this for the car salesperson. "My name is Mike and I work with Competitive Motors. We've found that there is a lot of confusion in the automotive market today because there have been over 150 new models introduced in just the past three years. I've developed a computer book that profiles everything the buyer wants in a car and in less than five minutes, identifies the models most likely to fit their needs."

Your Statement of Competitive Advantage

Mike has given his prospect a *statement of competitive advantage*. It has four components:
- your name
- your company
- a statement about a problem in your market
- how you and your product solve that problem

The statement of competitive advantage is a 30-second statement of what differentiates you in the marketplace.

Here's another example. "My name is Marlene and I work with a company called 'The Prescription for Doctors.' Physicians today are being pressured by insurers, employers, and patients to cut health care costs. Yet overhead costs for physicians are constantly rising. We provide a service that allows the physician to spend more time with patients and cut overhead costs at the same time resulting in better quality care at a lower cost. It's just what the doctor ordered!"

Here's one last example. "My name is Beth. It's nice to meet you. I'm with a company called 'The Greatest Advertising Agency in the World.' We've discovered that almost every successful product has either been the first entry in its category or it has been able to create a new category in the mind of its customers. What we do is help companies who are launching new products or having trouble with old ones ensure that their product is positioned to win!"

That really does set you apart from the competition. And it makes you sound like a polished expert right from the start. But how do you determine exactly what your competitive advantage is? The best way to determine your competitive advantage is to break down the components of your product or service into four distinct categories: competitive uniquenesses, competitive advantages, competitive parities, and competitive disadvantages. Let's look at each one individually.

Determining Your Competitive Advantage

Competitive uniqueness: means what can I do for my customers that no one else can do? What can I offer that no one else can offer?

Competitive advantage: is what can I do for my customer that my competitor can also do, but I can do it better and I can prove it?

Competitive parity: means objectively speaking my competitors and I are the same here—no real differentiation.

Competitive disadvantages: when you honestly answer the question: Where does the competition have an advantage over me?

You may want to do your analysis by market segment, competitor, by product or include all of them, but knowing your competitive position will quickly get you out of the pit and on your customer's wavelength.

An example of *competitive uniqueness* exists if a pharmaceutical company receives FDA approval to sell a new drug. Since no one else has the drug, this company now has a competitive uniqueness with this drug.

An example of a *competitive advantage* might be where two companies market the same drug, but one is a large well-known company and the other is a small relatively unknown company. Even though both are selling essentially the same product the larger company has an advantage because it's well known and people ask for the drug by its company name because of its wide name recognition. If no real competitive advantage exists in your product, try to focus on your company reputation, your excellent service, your responsiveness and reliability or any other factors than can positively differentiate you from your competition.

Next let's look at *competitive parity*—what things are the same between the competition and us? That is, what do you have that is exactly like what the competition has but is still important to the customer? Birth control pills are a good example. Several ethical drug companies make different formulations, but all with similar records for preventing pregnancy. This is competitive parity.

And finally, *competitive disadvantages*—what specific disadvantages does your product or service possess? That is, what does the competition do better than you do? Your drug may have more side effects than the competitor's. That's a competitive disadvantage.

In the examples we've just given, we were talking about the whole product as being unique or the same. But what do you do if you have a product where some features may be unique, some may be advantages, some may be the same and some may be disadvantages. Say for example, that you are selling a fax machine that uses plain paper—that's *parity*, because others do too. But maybe yours is the only one that will interface with phone, computer or car telephone—that's *uniqueness*. Yours also has the highest resolution available, that's an *advantage*, 300 number memory, another *advantage*, but it will not do broadcasting and polling, that's a *disadvantage*.

Here's an example in a service business. Federal Express will get it there over night, but so will other companies, so that's parity, by ten-thirty (used to be an advantage but now others are doing it so it has become a parity). But FedEx has a provable better track record, an advantage, and they can tell you in real time, exactly where your package is, that's a uniqueness. (Of course, in the rapidly changing world of service businesses, some of these benefits may have changed from advantages to parity, or vice versa, by the time you read this.)

We can't stress enough the importance of doing this analysis and knowing your competitive advantage. By doing this analysis you'll be in a position to help your customers distinguish between you and your competition. Once they see your uniquenesses and advantages, it will be easier for them to make a decision in your favor. In order to discover your competitive advantage, you may have to do some intelligence gathering—

- talk to your customers,
- talk to other salespeople,
- watch the local newspapers,
- attend tradeshows,
- talk to your customers' suppliers,
- build a file of your competitor's marketing and product information,
- do a debriefing when you lose a customer to a competitor,
- use a clipping service to gather information on competitors or on major prospects,
- obtain annual and quarterly reports of your competitors and prospective customers,
- watch the market trends in your industry and in your customers' industries,
- become the expert on your product or service and how it can help your customers.

Avoiding Price Focus

How many times have you been in a selling situation where the customer's sole focus was on price? Anytime your customers can't tell the difference between your product or service, and your competitor's, they will buy on price. You must differentiate your company, your product, your quality, your service, and yourself if you want the customer to stop focusing on price and start seeing you as a partner and not just as a supplier. You've got to show him how you are different.

I'm sure you can see now, why it's so important to know what you have to offer that's unique. But you may be wondering what you'll do with that information once you have it? How will you get it across to the client? You're going to use this information in every step of the sale. Your entire sales effort will be built around your competitive strengths. When you are targeting your market, you'll be looking for those clients whose needs are most likely to match your uniquenesses and advantages. When you contact clients, you'll open the conversation by letting them know what you can do for them that no one else can do. During the exploring phase, you'll be asking questions that will uncover client needs in the areas where you have uniquenesses and advantages. When you are collaborating with your client, you'll keep him focused on your uniquenesses and advantages and show him how they match his needs. During the commitment phase, you'll be summarizing all of the competitive advantages that your product has to offer and during the assuring phase, you'll be measuring how well your uniquenesses and advantages are serving your customer.

Let's summarize the two powerful strategies we've talked about so far that will give you THE COMPETITIVE ADVANTAGE. First, know what your competitive advantages and uniquenesses are, and second, be able to articulate them clearly to prospective customers in thirty seconds or less, in your statement of competitive advantage. This is your powerful opening to your targeted prospects... that all-important first impression that sets you apart from your competition. The next chapter will help you identify and target the prospects who are most likely to need your particular competitive advantage.

CHAPTER 2

IDENTIFYING AND FINDING
YOUR BEST CUSTOMERS

▼

Now that you know how to identify and state your competitive advantage, how can you identify those customer's who are most likely to want to hear your message? And once you've identified the profile of those most likely to buy, where can you find customers who fit your profile in large numbers?

Unless you are just starting in sales, look to your existing customer base for clues. Your current customers can point the way to others who might purchase in the future, because you'll probably find that your existing customers and your best potential customers have similar demographic and psychographic profiles. By demographics we mean that they have similar incomes, occupations or educational levels, are in the same industries, have similar structures or distribution systems, hold the same position within the company, etc. By psychographics we mean that they share similar beliefs, attitudes, values, priorities, and buying patterns.

Here's a good example of how you might use demographic profiling of your existing customers to help you find new customers. Suppose a review of your most profitable accounts shows that you've had success in the past selling your computer system to multi-branch banks. It would make sense to keep calling on multi-branch banks and to place a higher priority on them than you would on hardware stores where you've never sold a system. You might build on that success by calling on organizations that have a similar structure in similar industries, such as multi-branch consumer lending companies.

Why Do Your Customers Buy?

If you were to go and ask those banks specifically why they bought from you and they responded by saying that they felt comfortable with you because of your reputation for 24 hour support, error-free software and your one-year money back guarantee, you would have the beginnings of some psychographic data, or in other words a profile of their *buying values*. To refine it a little bit more you might ask them to reduce their reason for buying to one word or one sentence. In this case they might say "reliability and peace of mind." When approaching other banks and consumer lending companies, you would then use reliability and peace of mind as your focus for talking about your competitive advantage and point to your reputation for 24 hour support, error-free software and your one-year money back guarantee as support for your claim of reliability and peace of mind.

How to Identify Your Best Customers

Don't just guess or assume. Look at your demographic and psychographic data. You may be surprised to find out that the customers you regard as major accounts aren't necessarily the volume leaders; high visibility doesn't always translate into high volume. And often you'll find that the high volume accounts aren't necessarily the high profit accounts. They may be discounted deeply or require more servicing than some smaller accounts. So your current best customers may not be your current biggest customers. So how do you identify your best customers? Your study should begin with an analysis of your sales over the last two to three years. If you are new to sales or to your company look to experienced salespeople or to your sales managers for help here. In your analysis, you'll look for three things...

• Who bought what?
• Exactly how did we find and sell those customers?
• Why did they buy what they bought?

First, you want to look at who bought what. Which customers accounted for your past sales? What products or services did they buy and how much did they buy? Which sales were the most profitable? Which ones had the shortest sales cycle? Take a close look at which industry and segment of the market these accounts are in. The United States Chamber of Commerce has a coding system for every industry group and subgroup as well. They are called SIC codes or Standard Industrial Classifications. Identify which SIC codes your best customers belong to. Your local reference librarian can help you. Your goal is to identify the patterns in your high-volume and high-profit customers— the ones who provided the most valuable business to your company.

It's sometimes strategically valuable to sell to a customer who might not be high-profit, but who is high-prestige. Sometimes a company wants an industry leader on its customer list because of their high profile in a given industry. The fact that the leader has selected you can influence others to do business with you as well.

Some companies want to build market share regardless of volume and profit. If your company's primary focus is on building market share, you'll want to target *all* the possible customers who could buy your product. Whichever factors you use, determine the profile of your company's best customers: Who bought what?

Customer Source Patterns

Next, look at the sources of your best customers. Exactly how was that business acquired? Where did the initial contact come from? Was it a referral, a cold call, a walk-in, a trade show lead, or was it in response to an ad or a trade journal article you wrote. Who handled it initially and who finally brought in the business? Look for *patterns!* Find out what you are doing that is working. Success leaves clues, so look for them. This will help you to focus on your highest leverage opportunities for reaching similar customers. If you can find a pattern in your existing customer profiles you should be able to find new customers who are likely to buy, by finding other companies who fit the pattern of your existing customers. After you've got a good profile of what your best customers look like and you've discovered the patterns that have brought you together successfully in the past, ask yourself where you can find lots more customers that fit your profile?

For business-to-business selling, you should always start with industry associations. There is an association for just about every imaginable industry group in this country. Your local reference librarian can help you find them, or you may want to check with the American Society of Association Executives (ASAE). Often associations are listed in the local phone book, or you may want to look in the directory for your state capitol or in Washington, D.C., for national associations. Because most of them have a state or national lobbying arm, you'll find they tend to cluster around government centers. You may also want to check out New York City or Chicago as well since many are headquartered there. Your local phone company can get you directories for any city. Your local phone book also lists mailing list brokers who can provide you with lists of companies by industry or SIC code and they can often provide phone numbers and key contacts as well.

For person-to-person selling, there are directories listing professionals, small business owners, affluent individuals, and so on. Other sources include list brokers, magazine subscribers and catalog mailing lists or customer lists from other companies. And don't forget to consider past clients who may not be current clients. Be sure to check with the census bureau. They now have the data from the 1990 census available in some very sophisticated yet useable formats. If you have a good customer demographic profile, they can pinpoint your customers right to a given street or neighborhood.

If you're working with a local target market, you might look at what civic or professional groups your customers belong to. Some groups, such as the Rotary Club or an association of professional business-women, will rent their membership list while others require you to join to get it. Take a look at what other related products your best customers might buy in conjunction with your products. Software and hardware, for instance, or printing services and graphic design or office furniture and carpeting. Is it possible for you to do a joint promotion or trade lists with a non-competitor who also sells to your target market? What trade journals do your best customers read? If you can write an article for one of your industry trade journals, you can establish your expertise in your area. Articles are an excellent way to publicize yourself. What do your best customers do in their spare time? If it's golf, maybe you could sponsor an outing or tournament? The questions you want to answer are: Where do people with the same demographics or psychographics, as my best customers, cluster? Where can I find large groups of them in one place?

Tip clubs, or networking clubs, are fun and effective ways to gain leads, increase your visibility, build your network and be perceived as an expert at the same time. The purpose of these groups is to make each member aware of the resources available from the other members. This type of give-and-take results in group synergism. Each person is able to bring to the group his or her area of expertise, centers of influence, social networks and business contacts. With everyone bouncing ideas off one another, a kind of professional kinetic energy develops in which everyone can gain information, cross-sell, obtain referrals and increase the drive to achieve. A tip club's membership usually consists of professionals, business owners, executives, managers and salespeople in numerous business categories such as advertising, banking, real estate, insurance, consulting, office products, printing, stockbrokers, travel agents and so on. The best tip clubs are generally limited to one member from each field of business. They usually meet once a week at breakfast or lunch. Each member is to bring at least one lead that will benefit other members. It might be a general lead like letting them all know a new hotel will be built in town, or it might be a specific referral to another salesperson. The best tip clubs are fairly large and have one salesperson from each of many categories. To find one in your area, ask other salespeople you know, check with your local chamber of commerce, or start your own. Your tip club will grow quickly if the leads are of good quality. It's a great forum to promote your business economically, efficiently and effectively. Your fellow members become your sales force because they are constantly looking for ways to help you expand your business and they can also become your customers too.

Finally, consider why the customer bought your product. What exactly is it about your product, service or company that makes it attractive to your best customers? Why are they buying from you and not your competitors? They may be buying because others they trust know you and buy from you. They may buy because of physical proximity. They may buy because your credit terms are favorable. Sometimes you'll find that it's just habit or that they are unaware of other suppliers. You need to ask to find out.

Whatever you find out is valuable information because it tells you how you can best represent your products and services to prospective customers and it will give you some insights into the ways your customers see you, your company and your products.

By now, you should have a clear picture of what types of buying preferences typify your "best" customers. This, then, allows you to identify prospects who fit that "best customer" profile. Using the criteria set forth in your analysis, you can identify potential buyers who are likely to have the same needs and might buy for the same reasons as your best current accounts.

There's one more common denominator to look for in this analysis when you're selling to the business market. Which contacts in the customers' organizations have you had the most success with? What position within the company do most of our first contacts and ultimate buyers hold? Is it the president, vice president of marketing, director of operations, director of M.I.S., purchasing manager, or someone else?

Identifying these key contacts will let you know to whom you should direct your selling efforts.

Every company is different. Sometimes it does make sense to go to the person most likely to *buy* your product, such as the purchasing department. But more often, it makes more sense to go to the highest level person in the company who recognizes the problem your product or service solves. In a small company, that might mean calling on the President or CEO. In a larger company, that might mean contacting someone at the executive level, a director or vice president. Keep in mind that in the selling process you'll need to meet the needs of gatekeepers, users, buyers, influencers and deciders but ultimately it's the decider who needs to say yes. Starting too low in the organization could be the kiss of death. The president or department head may not be the one who places the order with you, but he can provide valuable information on the company and he can tell you whom you need to see to get action. Besides, what better way to get in to see the purchasing manager than to say the President referred you?

Summing Up

Let's review what we've covered so far. To find those common denominators that make up your "best customer" profile, identify who bought what, how exactly how you got those customers and why they bought what they bought from you. The answers to these three questions will help you target your best potential customers that will increase your likelihood of success. It will also help you to start thinking about segments of the market that you may not have thought about before. So far in the targeting step of sales, you've learned how to determine your competitive advantage and how to articulate it succinctly. You've also learned how to identify your best current customers and create a profile for the kinds of prospects you want to go after. In the next chapter you will find out how to use personal marketing techniques to generate a regular supply of qualified leads.

CHAPTER 3

USING PERSONAL MARKETING TO GENERATE LEADS

▼

Now that you can state your competitive advantage and know where to find high quality prospects, you need to know how to generate leads. We use a simple but very effective two-step approach: First, we'll show you ways to gain visibility with your best potential customers through personal marketing so that they will contact you. Second, we'll look at ways that you can make effective contact with prospective customers. We call the first method incoming and the second one outgoing.

Let's define both methods first before discussing them. If you make a cold call on a prospective customer, that would be outgoing because you initiated contact with the customer. If you were to run an ad and the customer called you in response, that would be incoming because the customer initiated the personal contact. And of course there are some gray areas in between. If you sent a direct mail letter and followed up on the phone, that's outgoing. If the customer called you before you got a chance to call her, that's incoming.

There are several reasons why making the distinction between outgoing and incoming is useful. First, you have a much higher degree of control over your outgoing efforts. You can run ads in a hundred publications, but if no one calls, you have no prospects. On the other hand, the quality of incoming leads is usually much higher. Since they called you, they are selecting themselves as a prospect for you, which usually means that they have an identified need and they want your help in determining if your product or service will fill their need. Let's first talk about how to get prospects to contact you.

Incoming Leads

At one time or another in our careers we've all known an experienced, successful sales rep who seems to just sit back and respond to calls.

The orders roll in and she seems to be getting rich without effort. What we generally don't see are the many years she spent paying her dues, building her sales network and investing in her personal visibility. She became synonymous with the product in the customer's mind. When they think of the product they think of her. She developed a reputation as an expert... and now she can benefit from those years of effort.

This successful sales person is using personal marketing. She's marketing herself just as a company would market a product. Just as it takes time to build brand loyalty, it takes time and hard work for personal marketing to pay off, but it's worth it in the long run. How you'll use these ideas depends to a large extent on where you are in your career. If you're just getting started you'll probably spend only five to 10 percent of your time on these methods because you'll need to focus more on outgoing prospecting activities covered later in this chapter. As your career and income grow, you'll want to invest more in these incoming methods until the majority of your customers are contacting you rather than the other way around. If your best potential customers have been made aware of you in advance of your contact with them through your personal marketing efforts, you'll find it much easier to establish a relationship with them, set up an appointment and consummate the sale.

The reason it's so important to invest at least some of your time in these methods right now, is that the quality of an incoming lead is almost always better than the quality of the lead you get on a cold call because the prospect has already identified himself as a probable candidate for your product. He's calling you because he has an identified need and he wants your help in determining if your product or service will fill it.

To gain high visibility and establish an aura of expertise, there are a number of strategies you can use:

Some of the most powerful sales and marketing tools available to you are your company website, a personal or company blog and podcasting. We are not going to delve deeply into these topics here because web marketing is not the focus of this book and space will not allow. But don't ignore these powerful tools. They can help you to create a local community of users or a global network of customers.

Let's discuss each of these visibility strategies so that you can use them more effectively in your selling efforts. We'll skip over personal selling because that's what this entire book is about. We'll also skip over direct mail because we devote the whole next chapter to it. So let's now discuss each of the remaining ten visibility strategies.

First, let's talk about personal advertising. You regularly see ads for products but rarely see ads by salespeople promoting themselves and their products except in the real estate industry. It's common there because they are independent reps and because they know that if they are going to get your listing, they have to be in your mind at the exact moment you are ready to sell your house.

If you want to have the competitive advantage in your industry or in your market area, you've got to think like an independent contractor. Depending on your target market and your company policy, you may want to run newspaper or magazine ads, or put your picture in the yellow pages.

Consider running a series of ads in a trade journal that's read by those people in your target market. You'll find that it can be very effective at building your image and making you a familiar face. Ask your customers in each industry category what trade publications they must read to keep up in their field. Almost every industry has at least one and some industries have many.

An idea that can be very powerful or a complete waste of money is advertising specialties. You're all familiar with the key chains and pens that companies give out with their names printed on them. There are literally thousands of ad specialty items available, but the key to using them is to find a gift your client will actually use or keep on his desk on a day to day basis that will be a powerful reminder of you and what you do.

One of the best examples we've seen of someone who has used this method well is George Walther, author of the book, *Phone Power*. In his seminars, George give away twenty-five-foot red, coiled telephone cords with an explanation that you should get up and move around while you're talking, to sound lively on the phone. People love them.

They run back to the office and put their red phone cord on their anything-but-red phone, and it really stands out. Whenever someone comes into their office, they ask, "Why do you have a red cord on your phone?" A discussion of the seminar and George Walther ensues, and suddenly George has a new seminar participant... who gets a red cord and... well, you get the point.

There are many practical options for generate incoming business through trade shows. The best way to identify what trade shows you should be attending is to ask your best customers which ones they attend. But there is a trick here. Be sure to ask them which ones they attend as a buyer or industry member as well as those in which they will be exhibitors. Each of these offers different opportunities for you. At those trade shows that your best potential customers attend as buyers or regular industry attendees, you can have a booth that might attract them to stop and examine your product or service offerings.

At those trade shows that your best potential customers attend as exhibitors, you can attend the trade show as a visitor and walk the floor stopping at relevant exhibit booths to learn more about your best potential customers' products and services. You'll also learn something about your customers' customers. You may even get to speak with some prospects who you haven't been able to contact yet. You may even make some sales. Trade shows are a great opportunity to see and speak with many of your best potential customers in one location in a short period of time.

Are we suggesting that you put up your own money to attend a trade show? Probably not, although if it's a local show you might want to consider it. What we're suggesting is that it's your responsibility to monitor all of the trade show activity for your particular territory and target market and work out a plan with your sales manager as to the best ways to leverage your opportunities at each show. At the very least, attend as a visitor and do some information gathering with the exhibitors. See if it would be profitable for you or your company to exhibit at this show next year. We attended the American Society for Training and Development trade shows before we ever decided to exhibit at it. We talked to various exhibitors, including some of our competitors, to determine if that trade show was a worthwhile investment of our limited marketing budget. Nearly everyone said it was a good investment, so we attended the following year as an exhibitor and made many sales as a result of our participation.

You could even participate in a joint promotion with a non-competitor. But this is something you would first want to consider with your sales manager. Let's say you sell business forms. Wouldn't it make sense to begin building a partnership with companies that sell computer printers? Why not start the relationships with a joint promotion where you promote their products to your existing clients and they promote your products to theirs? To look for possible selling partners, just think about all of the related but non-competitive products or services that are used in conjunction with yours.

Join an association in your best target market industry. This helps you find out about trends and issues important to your best customers. Also, contact other related trade associations for their membership list. Participate on committees to 'rub elbows' with the centers of influence in your key target industries.

Many people believe that public relations is supposed to be done by their company's ad agency or PR firm. For your company's products, that's probably true. But remember we're talking about your *personal* public relations campaign—getting your face and name known in the community. Any community involvement counts. Consider joining a club or association, for example, or doing volunteer work. The United Way has a loaned executive book that enables you to meet and work with some of the top executives in your area. It's a real opportunity to build your network. You'll find almost all of the local non-profit organizations are run by the movers and shakers in your community, but don't volunteer just for the business contacts. Do it for the personal growth it'll provide and the connection with your community that you will feel. The business contacts will take care of themselves.

Keep in mind that you want to join a local or national organization where you are likely to find people who fit the profile of your best customers. If your objective is to gain an identity in your target market nationally, a local group may not help much. Don't confuse activity with results. For salespeople who want to reach the affluent market for estate planning products or luxury goods and services, you might consider joining a fund raising group for the local symphony, opera or theatre. Many wealthy people actively participate in these groups or are the fund raising targets for these groups.

Publicity is aimed at generating favorable news coverage for you, your company and your products. You do not pay for publicity, at least not directly. You can write press releases about yourself, (perhaps your recent promotion) or your company (introducing a new product, for example) and send it in to the local newspaper, directed to the business section. You might even write a column in a target trade journal, magazine, newsletter or newspaper, or even letters-to-the-editor, to generate positive visibility.

Another way to get involved in civic and professional organizations is as a guest speaker. This is great way to reach a large number of prospective customers in a short period of time. But remember, as a speaker, your goal is to educate, not to sell. You want to make them enlightened buyers and you want them to recognize and remember you as the expert in this field so that when they are ready to buy, they come to you.

Another good way to raise your visibility and establish yourself as an expert, in addition to giving speeches, is to conduct free or nearly free seminars or workshops. This method has worked very well in the brokerage industry where investors and potential investors are invited to a free seminar on how to structure a portfolio or how to do technical stock analysis or to hear a famous investment guru speak. Attorneys and accountants have also found do-it-yourself seminars to be very profitable because once the attendees see the complexity of the issues involved they'll often ask the expert to just do it for them. One of our friends is a financial advisor in San Diego. One of his best markets is doctors. He frequently speaks at their meetings on financial planning strategies. They're constantly calling him to help them with their financial planning because his speaking engagements have given him the visibility of an expert.

Even if they don't contact you right away, you'll still be establishing your image as an expert. An ironic example of how this sometimes works is an experience we had with a local college. The college scheduled us for a seminar and mailed over ten thousand flyers to local businesses. An executive from one of the businesses called and engaged us to do extensive work with them. The ironic part is the original seminar was cancelled.

Tip clubs, or networking clubs, are also great ways to gain leads, increase your visibility, build your network and be perceived as an expert at the same time. The purpose of these groups is to make each member aware of the resources available from the other members. This type of give-and-take results in group synergism. Each person is able to bring to the group his or her area of expertise, centers of influence, social networks and business contacts. With everyone bouncing ideas off one another, a kind of professional kinetic energy develops in which everyone can gain information, cross-sell, obtain referrals and increase the drive to achieve. A tip club's membership usually consists of professionals, business owners, executives, managers and salespeople in numerous business categories such as advertising, banking, real estate, insurance, consulting, office products, printing, stockbrokers, travel agents and so on. The best tip clubs are generally limited to one member from each field of business. They usually meet once a week at breakfast or lunch. Each member is to bring at least one lead that will benefit other members. It might be a general lead like letting them all know a new hotel will be built in town, or it might be a specific referral to another salesperson. The best tip clubs are fairly large and have one salesperson from each of many categories. To find one in your area, ask other salespeople you know, check with your local chamber of commerce, or start your own. Your tip club will grow quickly if the leads are of good quality. It's a great forum to promote your business economically, efficiently and effectively. Your fellow members become your sales force because they are constantly looking for ways to help you expand your business and they can also become your customers too.

Newsletters can be an excellent personal marketing tool. The key is to make them valuable to the reader... not just a sales message disguised as a newsletter. If the newsletter is full of stuff that's interesting only to you, it won't get read. But if it's full of must-know product or industry information, it will be read and saved. Keep it short. If you make it too long, it will be put aside. Don't forget to include some cartoons and pictures for variety.

Now we come to one of our favorites... publish an article in a trade journal that your best potential customers might read. It immediately establishes you as an expert because an outside source (the trade journal) has recognized you as an expert. Besides getting you the initial exposure, you can use it as part of your personal brochure when you meet new clients, or you can use it as a direct mail piece. Many publications pay an honorarium for each article they publish. What we often do is exchange the honorarium for an ad in the same issue where our article appears. It's a one-two punch that really increases visibility and sales.

After you've written several articles, you can even turn them into a book. If you can't interest a publisher, self publish it. It'll really enhance your credibility as an expert in your field. Publishing a book may sound like an unattainable goal for most salespeople, but it's not as difficult as most people think. Talk to someone who's already been published to get some guidance. Tony just wrote a book with Garry Schaeffer titled Publish and Flourish: How to Boost Visibility and Earnings Through a Publishing Strategy. If you want to take advantage of a publishing strategy in your own field, get a copy of Tony's book and make it become a reality.

You may be wondering what you could write about? To get a better idea of where your book lies, answer these questions: What do you know well? Where are you an expert? What questions do your customers and prospects ask regularly? If they are confused maybe others in their situation are, too. There's a computer software and accessories company on the East Coast whose ads answer common customer and prospect questions. These ads are extremely effective lead generators.

Whatever sources you use, the key to good lead generation is *planning*. Remember that generating leads is a long-term activity that must be continuous if you are to be a successful salesperson.

Have a Plan

To make sure that your visibility strategies are all working together, you'll need a plan. You need to look at what you'll do to gain visibility with each of your target market segments. And put your plan in writing. Evaluate the plan from time to time and update it. You'll get great results with some activities, less with others. So periodically, examine and re-evaluate the plan... build on what works and modify what doesn't. Remember the whole point is to get your customers calling you!

Keep in mind that it's better to work on getting multiple exposures to a smaller target group than to spread your efforts and have fewer exposures to more people. Potential customers in your target markets should be...
- reading your articles,
- receiving direct mail from you,
- hearing you speak or giving a seminar,
- bumping into you at a social function or trade show, and
- hearing about you and your expertise from their fellow association members and friends in the form of referrals and testimonials.

Targeting a market means that you focus your limited marketing budget on those market segments most likely to buy from you so you'll get more "bang for the buck". When you effectively use these personal-marketing ideas, you'll find that little by little, people will start to recognize your name, your company, your product and your face. Pretty soon the phone will start to ring for you, and your image as an established expert will take hold. That's the power of personal marketing... and it's one more COMPETITIVE ADVANTAGE for you!

Outgoing Prospecting

As you gain this personal visibility and establish long-term customer relationships, incoming leads and customer referrals will come your way, but you can't sit back and wait for them. Part of your monthly routine must include outgoing prospecting. There are numerous ways to uncover new markets and establish new business contacts. There is no "best" strategy. They all work, so find the ones that work best for you, your product, your company and your industry. One of the many sources of prospects includes Satisfied Customers. These are people with whom you have business relationships. They should be systematically contacted to see if additional needs exist. Satisfied customers are such an easy market to reach that they frequently slip through the cracks. Keep in mind different departments, divisions, parent companies and other spin-offs of your present customers. In addition, when your company introduces new products or services, your entire customer list becomes a prospect list. At least once a year you should go through your customer list and a list of your products and services to see if new opportunities exist.

Company Leads are another excellent source. Often your company will provide leads from ads, direct mail responses, telephone campaigns and other valuable sources. These leads are generally high quality because the prospect has already expressed an interest in your company. In this case, don't procrastinate; get back to the prospect quickly.

Centers of Influence are prominent people in your community who can direct you toward new prospects. A center of influence may be a priest, rabbi, minister, congressperson, attorney, banker or influential business-person. Focus on building a trusting relationship with them before asking for referrals. Be sure they know the benefits you have provided other customers. Let them know your goals so they can be aware of the kind of prospects you're looking for. Give them a formal presentation describing your product or service. Provide them with an extensive list of testimonials, personal and business references, and a professional resume. Centers of influence are only interested in referring those salespeople who will not undermine their reputations. Be sure to report back to the center of influence after you contact the person they referred to you. And finally, find a professional way to reciprocate or to say "thank you."

Orphan Accounts. These are former customers who, for some reason, have stopped buying. Often it's because the salesperson who was handling their account has left the company or they may have stopped doing business with the company because of a product or service problem. If you can solve the problem, you have a good chance of winning back the account for yourself. These accounts represent a gold mine right under your nose.

There are innumerable directories to the businesses in your industry and geographical location. The local library and chamber of commerce are invaluable resources. If you are not familiar with their directories and indexes, ask for help.

Prospects are everywhere. Be observant. Keep your eyes, ears and mind open to the people and situations around you. You never know when your expertise will be needed.

Whether you are using incoming or outgoing prospecting techniques, create a system for monitoring and measuring your prospecting efforts. The more organized you are, the less likely you are to lose names and numbers, forget about prospecting or make other costly mistakes. The first step is to get a file and, if necessary, help in setting it up. Keep track of everything about the prospect including dates of contact, who referred you, possible needs or opportunities and so on.

Your system should have steps to take for each prospect. You'll need to do a minimal amount of research to identify those who will be most promising. To organize your client and prospect files, consider this system:

- Use a hanging file system with 8 1/2 X 11 file folders.
- Label 26 of the files A–Z. These will be your master files for your client list. You can either have a separate master prospect file or, if there is room, combine them with present clients.
- Give each client its own page and record all the permanent information you have on the company, the decision-maker, your contacts, addresses, phone numbers, birthdays, spouses names, everyone's hobbies, the dog's name and hobbies and so on. Attached to this master sheet will be a contact report. Every time you talk to this client, make a note of the reason, outcome and date of your next contact.

To remember when to contact customers, set up a tickler file. You probably have one already, but consider improving it with some of our ideas. You can use a notebook, several notebooks or a small card file. Whatever system you use, it should be divided into twelve months. There should also be a section for the current month and it should be divided into four or five weeks. For each client or prospect there will be an index card on which you will write the client's name and contact date. As you plan contacts and follow-ups, simply put the cards in the appropriate week. At the end of each week, spend some time reviewing the up-coming week's calls and put those cards in your daily reminder, notebook or daily tickler file.

After you contact a customer, enter your notes on the contact report and put the tickler file card in the week of the next contact. There is a good reason to keep your master files and tickler files separate. Imagine you are in your office and a client calls. You have to quickly dig up your information on the account. If that information is in alphabetical order in the master file, you know exactly where to look. If it were attached to the tickler card and filed under a date somewhere in the future, you would not know where to find it unless you happened to remember when you were going to recontact that person.

Setting up a system like this may seem like a headache, however, it is worth the effort. There are also some alternatives. You could solicit the help of a well-organized friend. You could use one of the many computer programs that will organize you. You could also work with a secretary who would take the paperwork off your desk and put it in files rather than piles. Your secretary would also update your files and keep you from interfering with the system. If you choose the latter idea, an efficient and timesaving tactic is to dictate the information and have it transcribed and filed.

Summing Up

No matter what system you use, it is absolutely essential to follow through with your prospects. Always keep the ball in your court. Don't expect them to call you back. If you spend the time to follow-through, you will find your appointment book filling up with new names and numbers.

Identifying your best prospects and setting up lead generation systems that provide you with a steady stream of prospects to talk to is the first step in the sales process. The next step is to Contact the prospects in a way that enhances your sales message. The next section will help you understand how to make each Contact with a prospect or customer more effective.

STEP II

CONTACTING

▼

Once we know how to identify prospective customers, we need to contact them with our message. When you come right down to it there are really only three ways to contact a potential customer—by mail, by phone and in-person. If you want to get fancy you could include telegrams, electronic mail and fax, but they're really just other forms of mail. Direct mail is an excellent technique for breaking the ice with a prospect and beginning to build an image of credibility and reliability. Direct mail can take the cold out of cold calling.

As the cost of in-person sales calls escalates, more and more salespeople are using the phone to reduce, and in some cases eliminate, costly face-to-face sales calls. Often the cost of personal visits isn't the problem as much as their ineffectiveness. When salespeople make appointments with prospects who turn out to be not so qualified, a great deal of time is wasted. Good phone skills combined with a well-structured direct mail program can provide you with high quality personal appointments that lead naturally to sales.

Once you've obtained an appointment with a golden prospect who meets all your criteria, you want that appointment to flow easily and effortlessly into an exploration of the prospect's needs and concerns. This flow depends on the quality of the relationship you build... which depends on your ability to understand how your prospect wants to be treated. Spending a great deal of time talking about family and hobbies to a fast-paced, task-oriented person can destroy all your prior efforts. The chapter on relationship strategies will help you know how to adapt your actions and communications to the needs of the person you are dealing with.

The old adage, "You never get a second chance to make a good first impression," is the truth behind the Contact stage. A successful sale is like building a pyramid—each step depends upon the success of the previous steps and no step can be left out without creating disaster.

CHAPTER 4

CONTACTING PROSPECTS WITH DIRECT MAIL

▼

The first contacting method we'll look at is direct mail. When we speak of direct mail, we're not talking about the huge mailings of hundreds or thousands of pieces that your company might send as part of their advertising program. These mailings generally do not involve personal or phone follow-up. The direct mail process we speak of as part of the Contact stage of sales includes a well-thought-out letter addressed to your best potential customers, with a phone follow-up.

Have you ever been in a sales slump? Sales are booming then all-of-a-sudden they fall through the floor. Most salespeople tell us that happens because they get so busy working with prospects, negotiating deals, and demonstrating the product or service, that they didn't have time to make contacts with new prospects. The sales pipeline emptied and there was no interested prospects left to work with! Almost all sales slumps are caused by the lack of a consistent system for prospecting.

The reason it works so well is that it keeps you from ever having to make a cold call again. While there are some salespeople who say they "love" cold calling, we found that most sales people approach cold calling in the same way most of us approach rattlesnakes and warts. Cold calling always involves a great deal of rejection and most of us want to avoid rejection, therefore, we avoid cold calling. Success in sales requires consistent prospecting... but that does not mean cold calling! By using the direct mail program described below, you can keep your sales pipeline full of interested prospects and avoid periodic sales slumps.

One of the first things you have to understand, however, is selective perception. Every day we are bombarded with thousands of messages. In order to keep us from going crazy with information overload, our brains filter out most of the messages and let through only those that trigger recognition or need. This filtering process is called selective perception and we all use it everyday. To demonstrate how selective perception works, let's use an experience that most of us have had. Think about the last time you began shopping for a car. As soon as you decided you were in the market for a car, you suddenly started noticing automobile ads everywhere—billboards, magazines, newspapers, and radio. It almost seemed you couldn't turn around without seeing a car ad. Then you picked out the car you wanted. Suddenly, you saw that same car... sometimes even the same color... everywhere. Everyone seemed to have one. Why hadn't you noticed before? Selective perception. Your brain was filtering these messages out until you decided you needed a car. Then your brain started to let in all those messages about cars.

How does the concept of selective perception apply to your use of direct mail? Well, most sales people send one piece of direct mail and hope that:

1. It gets read
2. It appeals to the reader's need and
3. That the reader will take action to get your product or service or will remember that they were interested by the time you get around to calling.

Don't bet on it! In a society saturated with advertising, fifteen seconds after they hear, or read, your message, they are being bombarded with the next message.

If they get the first letter and it passes through their need filter... Great! They'll call you! But what if they don't?

Let's take a look at what typically happens. Your prospect gets your letter, glances at it, and throws it away. Say you send a follow-up letter. The prospect gets it and says (unconsciously) "I've heard of this guy someplace before." Assume that you understand marketing and psychology enough to send a third letter. The prospect says, "You know, I've heard a lot about this company. Maybe I should give them a call."

You bet they've heard a lot about this company! And it has all been good because they've heard it all from *you!* So what happens when you call and ask for an appointment? You're credible. You're not just another sales person. You're a consultant with expertise in a field in which they now have an interest. Studies have repeatedly shown that when a person hears about *you*, your *company* or your *product* four or more times, they perceive you as credible. Our direct mail system sets you up as an expert so you can make warm calls on hot prospects, which beats cold calling any day of the week!

To begin, send three different letters, one week apart, to each prospect. Then call for an appointment three to five days after the last letter. This direct mail strategy might sound overwhelming as a general prospecting tool but it can be used quite successfully by using it with the top 10% of your best prospects, the ones who can deliver up to 80% of your sales volume and profit. This ideal group of prospects is well worth the time, money and effort of this highly successful direct mail technique.

Every day select four new prospective customers from your target market with whom you have never spoken and send them letter number one. This is the magical part of the system that ensures you'll always have a fresh supply of prospects.

Let me caution you here. Sales people, being ever optimistic, often say, "Well, if four per day is good, a hundred a day is better!" And soon find themselves so far behind on their calls that by the time they get around to following up, the prospect has forgotten about the letters. Another reason to send only four is that even during your busiest season, there is no excuse for not following up on your four new prospects for that day. This is a system that takes only a few minutes a day and has tremendous payoffs.... *But you must work the system every day.*

Those of you who are quick at math have already figured out that after the first couple of weeks you will be sending out twelve to sixteen letters each day. You will be sending letter one to new prospects, letter two to last weeks prospects, letter three to the prospects from two weeks ago, etc. In a few minutes, I'll tell you how to set up a system on your personal computer or word processor so the whole process will take only a few minutes a day, but first let's talk about the direct mail piece itself.

First of all, make it look personal. What does personal mail look like? It is addressed by hand or typewriter—not with a mailing label. It is preferably hand stamped. Using a postage meter immediately identifies it as business mail, but is acceptable today because it is in such widespread use. Personal letters either has no return address or has just the address but not the company name and logo. The return address should also be typed or handwritten. For a little twist, use a simple address printed on the back flap.

Making it look personal ensures that it gets opened, but how do you make sure it gets opened *first?* Make it lumpy! Why? The prospect gets his mail and says, "What could that lump possibly be? It must be a gift... for me!" Why would they want to open bills when they could be opening presents? They always open it first or last and in either case you've got their undivided attention! How do you make your mail lumpy? Include a cassette, a video, an advertising specialty, or a sample of your product. It doesn't really matter as long as it's related to your message.

How about the layout and copy of the actual letter? Well, you're going to use the same statement of competitive advantage that you developed earlier. Whenever you are introducing yourself to a client, regardless of whether it's in person, on the phone or by mail, you are going to use the same basic positioning statement or a variation. Here are a couple of examples:

Sample letter #1

What Do Xerox, IBM and Mercedes Benz Have in Common?

Dear _____:

They all use the Herald Newspaper to enhance their image throughout the San Diego area... and increase their overall sales.

They've told us that our extensive circulation coupled with the high quality of our subscribers makes us the most effective medium in San Diego County for their advertising dollar.

If you would like to discuss some strategies for getting our readers into your store, please call me at 123-4567.

Sincerely,

Rick Barrera

P.S. Our upcoming real estate issue may be of special interest to you. It will be out the first week of December.

Sample letter #2

Your Kids Can Be the Most Popular Kids on the Block!

Dear _____:

Have you ever noticed how kids just naturally gravitate to certain homes in your neighborhood? It seems like there's always one house that is sort of a kid magnet. Why is that?

Perhaps its' the parents, the location, a big yard, or maybe that there's always something to do at that house... but whatever the reason there is a big payoff to the parents and to the kids who live there.

It's the development of social skills. A Carnegie Foundation Study showed that 85% of success in life comes from our ability to deal effectively with other people, so the earlier we learn these important skills, the better off we are.

Give your kids the edge. Make your house the neighborhood center with a Sunshine Playground.

Sincerely,

Tony Alessandra

P.S. There's an even bigger benefit to you. You don't ever have to wonder where your kids are!

I'm sure you noticed that we used a headline and included a P.S. Research has shown that most people will read the headline and the P.S. before any other parts of the letter. They are the prime locations of your message so always put a stand alone benefit message in the headline and a related benefit message in the P.S. By stand alone, we mean that if the prospect just read the headline and the P.S., he will get a complete message about your company, your product or you. It's important that the reader is able to scan the letter and determine what the product or service is and what the offer is. It's also important to have a call to action. Remember that your primary objective is recognition.

Your direct mail is only limited by your imagination. If you think your letters are fun and focused on creating opportunities or solving problems for your clients, odds are your prospects will too. If you think they are dull, so will your clients. Write several sample letters and ask three of your current customers who match your target audience to read and critique them. Use their feedback to make changes because they'll be your best predictors of the actual results you'll get with your direct mail book.

Always include a postage-paid reply card to make it easier for the prospect to respond. Always include a toll free or local phone number so the prospect can respond. With the new toll-free services available, any size business can now have toll-free service *without* adding any additional lines. Be sure to print the toll-free number on the reply card as well as on the cover letter. People will often reach for the reply card to respond and then realize it's easier just to call.

Organizing Your Direct Mail System

Now we'll show you how to make the whole system work with a minimum of hassle. If you have a computer, type in each of your three different prospecting letters. If you don't have a computer, find a printer or secretarial service that does. Then enter your 80 new prospects' names and addresses into your computer. (That's four per day times twenty working days in a month.)

Print out all 240 letters at once but stagger the dates you print on the letters so that they can be sent out on the appropriate dates. (If you are using a database computer program, the three dates can be added to the prospect's data record. If you're not, it will take a little time to stagger the dates for all 240 letters but it makes the rest of the month extremely simple.) Stuff all of the envelopes and seal them. But before you seal them, write the date that is printed on the letter on the upper right hand corner of the envelope where the stamp goes. Then, each day all you need to do is to pull all of the envelopes with today's date, put stamps on them, and drop them into the mail. To make the phone follow-up easier, print out a list of prospects with the date they received letter number three so you know what date to call.

That's it! Our simple system for creating an on-going stream of high quality prospects. Let's review the key points:

1. Send three different letters to each prospect, one week apart.
2. Mail to four new prospects every single day.
3. Make it look personal.
4. Make it lumpy.
5. Always include a headline and a P.S.
6. Always include a reply card and a toll free number
7. Follow up by phone three to five days after your last letter.
8. Computerize your system for ease and efficiency and work it every day.

Direct mail systems don't work overnight, but they do work over time. For some businesses it can take six months or more before you see the real benefits of this effort. Be patient and you will be handsomely rewarded. And, don't forget that direct mail is not a science, it's an art. So test everything you do to see what works for you. You may not need to send three letters. You may get the same results with one or two... or it may take you four. You may get the same results with or without the lumps. Experiment! Have fun! The system can't possibly work if you don't use it. So get started today!

CHAPTER 5

GETTING AN APPOINTMENT

▼

Once your prospective customers have received your letters, you'll need to follow up on the phone. The telephone is potentially your most efficient and profitable marketing tool. When you are selling on the phone, you don't have time to waste. You must be a polished professional. For that reason, we're going to go back to the basics that most salespeople get out of the habit doing. Vince Lombardi, the late, great coach of the Green Bay Packers, used to say to his champion teams on the first day of practice, "Gentleman, this is a football." We'll start the same way: "Salespeople, this is a telephone." Learning how to use it effectively will increase your income and give you another competitive advantage!

As a professional salesperson, you prepare before going to meet with a prospect in person. You do some research on him and his company. You plan your strategy and prepare some questions to ask. You make sure you have your competitive advantage, or initial benefit, statement ready and you have familiarized yourself with some key phrases or jargon that demonstrate your understanding of the prospect's industry. You have thought through any initial resistance he might bring up and have facts, studies or references ready to help him past those resistances. So why should the phone be any different? Unfortunately, for many salespeople, it is different. They find a prospect's name, pick up the phone and "wing-it." Then they say, "Telemarketing isn't as effective as face-to-face sales calls."

How to Get Your Prospect on the Phone

While phone calls don't have the advantage of being able to see the prospect's environment and they don't give you the chance to make as much of a personal impression, they can be a highly effective part of your sales process. Preparing for the telephone call just as you would the in-person call will make a big difference in your results. Each time a prospect gets on the phone with you, you have an opportunity to create a new lifetime customer. Being prepared ensures that you will maximize that opportunity.

Being effective on the phone includes finding out who the best person is to speak with, getting them on the phone, and then engaging them in your idea in such a way that they'll want to learn more in a face to face meeting. And remember, if you miss on any of the three, you're out. That's why absolute proficiency in this area is critical.

One of the best ways to get someone to take your call is to call the company and ask to speak with the president's secretary. Ask her for the name of the person who is responsible for making an executive level decision for your type of product or service.

Then, call that person and use the president's secretary's name during your introduction. Another good way to get through the company screen is to call the switchboard and ask for the direct dial number of the person you are calling and call back his extension.

Call before or after regular business hours, or at lunchtime. Many executives go in early or stay late. You'll often find the assistant isn't there to screen the call. At lunchtime, you'll find a fill-in who generally won't screen the call... and don't forget to try Saturday mornings when many executives are in.

Many salespeople make the mistake of hanging up on voice mail. It's an opportunity to speak directly to your potential customer at a time when he is ready to hear it. Pay close attention to the personality and style of the outgoing message he leaves and match his style and pacing in your message. Give your name, company and number first, then your message and your name and number again so he won't have to replay your message to get the number.

If your lead is a referral, ask the person who referred you to make a call on your behalf to set an appointment or perhaps you could try a conference call so they could tell the prospect why they are recommending you.

What do you do if you get your prospect's assistant? Asking if the person is an assistant, rather than a secretary, will get the relationship off to a good start. Make the assistant your ally. Find out his or her name; show respect; tell the assistant your situation and ask for their help. Ask for the person by first name only in a very casual manner.

The assistant may perceive you as a personal friend and not bother to screen the call. But never lie. Don't say, "it's personal" if it isn't. State your name and company clearly. Give the reason for your call. If you initially sent a direct mail letter, you might say that you are following up on correspondence you sent recently and that the prospect is expecting your call. The prospect should be since you stated in your direct mail letter that you would be following up by phone.

Be sure to acknowledge that you are concerned about not wasting the boss's time. You're calling to spend just a minute or so on the phone to determine if any further follow-up is needed. If now isn't a good time, when does the assistant think might be convenient? Would it be possible to make a phone appointment at that time?

If your prospect isn't in when you call, find out when she'll be in and call back. If you're really having a hard time getting through, try the fax. Most offices don't have a procedure yet for screening faxes. But make the fax message a short statement of benefit and a request for a phone or personal appointment. Do not send multiple page messages or brochures by fax... it ties up your prospect's fax machine and can be very irritating.

If it looks as if you're really not going to get through, you may want to ask the assistant for the names of others inside the company who might be open to your ideas. If you can get a foot in the door, you may be able to build alliances with them that will get you an audience with the key decision-maker.

If everything else has failed and this is an important enough customer, consider sending your prospect a check made out to her favorite charity with a letter stating that if she'll meet with you for a few minutes, you'll sign the check.

If you really want to get creative, you can send flowers or balloons to your prospect with a note saying "I have an idea that will send your business sky high" or "I'm sure our relationship would bloom if we could speak for a few minutes." Use your imagination and have some fun. If you've done your homework and know that your product or service would have benefit for this prospect, these creative approaches can pay big dividends.

Remember to watch your investment of time, energy and money, because it might make more sense to just move on to another prospect. We have a rule: three calls and a letter or fax, then try something creative or follow up in three to six months. Things may have changed dramatically by then.

It's also important to remember the purpose of your call is not to make a sale; it's to begin building a long-term relationship. You want an appointment so you can get to know your prospect and her needs.

We also recommend you monitor and measure your calls. To improve any skill, you need a baseline to which you can compare your progress. To increase your effectiveness on the telephone, keep track of your calls. A telephone log will help you structure the data you should keep on each calling session. This log is not concerned with individual accounts. It is a day-by-day tally of what happened with each call you made.

The importance of keeping a log is in the analysis of the results. Let's say, for example, you chose a different time to make your calls every day for two weeks. At the end of that time, your log would show you which times were productive and which were not. If you found you had to call a customer an average of three times before getting through, you may be calling at the wrong time. If you find you're getting through to your prospects, but not getting results, you should analyze your telephone habits. Without a telephone log, you won't be able to see the patterns and analyze your performance.

Objections = Avoidance Tactics

Now let's discuss those upfront objections you receive like "I'm not interested... or I'm happy with my current supplier." Most upfront objections are avoidance tactics. The prospect doesn't want to talk to you because he's afraid you are going to pressure him. His way of avoiding the pressure is to hit you with upfront objections that he hopes are difficult to counter.

If you have done a good job targeting your prospects, you know there is a good chance your product or service would be interesting to your prospect. So you need to get past those upfront objections. Open with your competitive advantage statement and be sure it contains a specific benefit for this customer. Suppose you're selling a cost accounting system for hospitals. You might say: "Our case mix management module is used by over 40% of the hospitals your size, and last year those hospitals reported savings averaging 18%." To make that introduction even more powerful, give him the name of someone who referred him.

A familiar name is a powerful icebreaker... especially if it's the name of a respected peer.

When the prospect says he has no need, you have to let him know you won't try to sell him anything unless you can clearly show how you can help him—help him increase profits, decrease costs or increase productivity. Let him know that the purpose of your call is to begin building a mutually beneficial business relationship and to learn more about him and his company so you can be more specific about the benefits he'll receive.

You might also say something like this: "It's funny you should say that. I just finished installing one of our systems for Ms. Collins at Oak Bridge hospital. Initially she didn't think she needed it either, but after we showed her the results of our free system review, she realized she did have a need after all. Could I offer you a free system review?"

If your prospect is too busy or has no time to see you now, you can ask to schedule an appointment at a more convenient time, or even ask for a phone interview. You might also promise not to take up any more time than he'll allow you. If at that point he wants you to leave, you will. But, if he wants you to stay longer to complete your collaborative sales process, you'll be more than happy to do so. The decision on how long you'll stay is totally dependent on him. As a sweetener you might also offer breakfast, lunch, dinner or a ride to the airport when he takes his next trip. Stress that you really do want to get to know him and his business a little better and that you're willing to go out of your way to do it.

What if your prospect has no time to see you at all? You might say that's exactly why he should take the time to see you. This statement should be used when you sell a product or service that is more convenient, can save time or make the prospect more efficient, such as a computer system, portable or mobile phone, dictation equipment, certain software, or a service that would free him of something he has to currently do himself, such as financial planning or recruiting new employees.

When you come across a prospect who's happy with her current supplier, you might ask, "Of all the things you like about your present supplier, what one thing do you like least?" Here you are looking for areas where you have a competitive uniqueness or advantage. The objective here is to have the prospect discover for herself some discontent with her existing supplier or product. That's where you can be of help. Make sure this doesn't come across as "competition bashing", but as an honest attempt to discover ways you can help this prospect achieve her goals better than her current supplier.

You can also talk about the merits of dealing with multiple suppliers for the same products. Offer to just update her on your most recent products and prices so she can keep her current supplier on their toes. You might say, "Most of my clients find competition among suppliers to be good business and an easy way to manage a vendor's service and price commitments. You may want to discuss how economic or political conditions, supply shortages, mergers, acquisitions, business failures, and so on dictate not relying on a sole supplier.

Making a Cold Call in Person

Now let's discuss approaching the prospect via an in-person "cold call"? Cold calling can be an excellent complement to your other forms of prospecting, especially when you're selling a product that has universal interest, such as office products or supplies, or in an area where prospects are highly concentrated, such as an office building in a major city or an office park in a small suburban area. You have the benefit of reaching many prospects in a relatively short period of time.

Many sales people say that they don't make cold calls. They respond only to company-supplied leads, advertising inquiries or referrals. But these sales people don't realize that every call they make on a new prospect is, in a sense, a "cold" call. When the sales person contacts the prospect, that prospect is very likely preoccupied with something else. The sales person must therefore help that prospect make a mental and physical transition from what they're doing now to what the sales person would like them to be doing and thinking. In cold call selling, the sales person may not only be competing with another company for that prospect's business, but more importantly, will very likely will be competing for that prospect's time and attention.

Some industries still use in-person cold calling quite effectively. For instance, we purchased a security alarm system for our home. Immediately after it was installed, the salesperson called on our neighbors to explain what kind of alarm signals they might hear. While he was offering information, he was also explaining their service and doing some very smart "cold call" selling. Cold calling is very effective when you have a product that appeals to universal needs, such as security alarm systems, office products and printing.

Even in industries where in-person cold calling is not the norm, salespeople often make drop in calls when they are in a certain vicinity and have time between appointments. A good example was my neighborhood real estate agent who represented a national real estate company. When I bought my first home in San Diego, she stopped by to welcome my wife and me to the area. She introduced herself as our neighborhood realtor. She explained her vast knowledge of the local market and told us about her network of contacts that made it easy for her to list and sell homes specifically in our neighborhood. Every month, without fail, she'd stop by our house to say hello and drop off a newsletter on trends in the local real estate market. Without fail, she'd always ask if we knew of anyone who might be interested in selling or buying a home. It took nearly 13 months, but when my wife and I were ready to sell our home and move up to a bigger one, we could think of no one better than this woman to sell our current home and to take us around to help us purchase our new home. She made two sales by persistent, friendly cold calls.

One of the reasons more sales people don't make cold calls is because of fear—typically a fear of rejection or a fear of making a fool of themselves. One of the best ways a sales person can avoid making a fool of himself is to be well prepared before making any cold calls. Knowing how to open the call to immediately create prospect interest is a good first step. Most of the techniques we discussed earlier are as true for in-person cold calling as phoning. You need to make sure your first 30 seconds includes a targeted positioning statement and whenever possible say who referred you. Never say, "I was just in the neighborhood." It sounds as if you had nothing better to do. Open with your positioning statement and then say "I had planned to call you next week but I was working with Mr. Miller at CXX right next door and we finished a little early so I thought I'd drop by to see if we might be able to set up an appointment.

Collaborative sales people do their homework prior to making cold calls. The more pre-call preparation the sales person does, the less fearful and threatening the sales call becomes. It's like turning a "cold" call into a "warm" call. Collaborative sales people plan and research their territories, their competitors and their best potential customer market segments before contacting a prospect for the first time. There are many benefits to Pre-call preparation. First, it saves time. Prospects appreciate it when you take up as little of their time as possible. Second, it makes you look professional. Being organized allows you to be informed and communicate quickly and effectively. Third, it reduces tension. Sales people who are well prepared worry less about things going wrong. Last, it increases your sales. The more prepared you are, the more effective you'll be in every cold call you make and the more sales you'll be able to make.

The preparation you do before cold calling should focus on which geographic area or type of business would be most receptive to cold calls. Once you determine the area and type of business to cold call, you'll then need to identify the specific prospects to call on—those who need your product and are able to buy. Before the initial cold call contact, you should uncover the name of the decision-maker you'll have to deal with at each specific company you'll be cold calling. This information can be obtained by calling a receptionist and asking, "Who is the person responsible for..." or "Who is in charge of..." You can also ask noncompetitive sales people who are familiar with the company the name of the key decision maker in that company. Other sources can be industry journals, annual reports and local business newspapers.

There are several steps that should be undertaken before you have cold call meetings with prospects. These steps focus your attention and creative energy and increase your success significantly. First, do all the research and preparation possible. Second, write out the questions you intend to ask as well as the general topics you plan to cover during the cold call. Third, anticipate the prospect's answers and brainstorm possible problems and opportunities that may arise. Fourth, visualize your success. Spend time sitting quietly with your eyes closed and imagine yourself with the prospect successfully achieving your objectives. This is a powerful tool that really works! Fifth, role-play in-person cold calls with fellow sales people. Many sales people avoid this exercise, but those who use it swear by it. Role-playing will sharpen your ability to anticipate questions and issues. Your role-playing partner should stretch your imagination without harassing you for the fun of it. It's also helpful to record your role playing session on audio or videotape. The insight you'll gain from listening or watching the session will be invaluable. Sixth, go over your cold call objectives, ideas, questions and overall plan of action with your sales manager. Get feedback and input as to how to improve your approach. Finally, sleep on it. You'll be amazed what you'll think of when you let all the information percolate in your mind. You'll think of additional questions, issues and creative ideas. This seven-step program of pre-call planning will serve you well if you use it routinely. Of course, for brief cold call meetings with prospects, you need only do some of the steps.

Just a reminder of something I'm sure you already know. It's essential to have everything ready and at your disposal when meeting with a prospect. Plan ahead. Take enough business cards, literature, brochures and other documents you may need. If you'll be riding in your car with the prospect, make sure it's clean. If you'll be giving a presentation, make sure your equipment is in top working order. Photocopied documents should be stapled and carried in something that will protect them. Giving forethought to your presentation will help you avoid embarrassing surprises.

Simply stated, preparation takes the fear and the unknown out of in-person cold calls and makes them a much more effective part of your entire selling process. Generally speaking, don't expect to make a sale on your very first cold call unless you're selling a relatively inexpensive widely used product, such as magazines, cleaning products, office supplies and the like. What you should expect to accomplish on your first cold call is to begin establishing a relationship with the key decision-maker and his or her assistant. You may also be lucky enough to gather some information about the prospect's needs and expectations that you can use to develop options and solutions for your next call.

Summing Up

You might be wondering which of the three contacting methods yields the best results—direct mail, telephone, or in-person cold calls. Most top salespeople use all three of the contacting methods in order to reach the largest number of qualified prospects possible. Each different sales situation will need its own mix of direct mail, telephone and in-person contacts. Use your judgment and your own past experience as a guideline.

The next chapter will help you understand how to tailor each of these contact methods to the particular preferences of your prospects. It will give you a simple guide to building strong relationships with your customers.

CHAPTER 6

RELATIONSHIP STRATEGIES

▼

We've given you numerous good ideas for contacting prospects through the mail, on the phone and in person. Now it's time to start building the face-to-face relationship with the prospect. As we said earlier: you seldom get a second chance to make a good first impression. So, how do you make sure when you begin the actual sales call that your first contact gets the relationship started right? Should you talk about the big football game or get right down to business? Unfortunately, many salespeople choose the option they're most comfortable with while accidentally ignoring the needs of the customer. If you treat others as you want to be treated, you may end up ignoring their needs, wants, and expectations that may be completely different from yours.

But how do you know how your prospects and customers want to be treated? To help simplify this critical task for you, we've developed a sales tool we call the Behavioral Style Grid. It will help you understand how to best deal with all the people in your life, especially your clients and prospects. The Behavioral Style Grid is constructed by understanding two dimensions of behavior. The first is indirect/direct.

Indirect ———————————————————————————— Direct

People on the direct side of the scale, the right hand side, are fast-paced people who make decisions quickly, like to take risks and are often impatient. *Indirect* people, on the left-hand side, operate at a slower, more deliberate pace. They are patient, make decisions more carefully and avoid risk.

Direct people come on strong, take the initiative and tend to be assertive and impatient. They tend to talk a lot and appear confident and emphatic. Indirect people are more reserved, quiet and sometimes appear indecisive when actually they merely avoiding the risk that might be involved in a poor decision. They are less confronting, demanding and assertive than the direct people. They are good team players and often let others take the initiative.

The other dimension is Supporting/Controlling.

Supporting

Controlling

Supporting people, on the topside of our behavioral grid, are open with their thoughts and feelings. They use a lot of body language and facial expressions and their conversations generally include a lot of stories and anecdotes. They are generally casual about time and are more interested in relationships than tasks. Their feelings play an important part in the decisions they make. If supporting people are "open books," controlling people are "poker faced." Controlling people, on the bottom of the grid, like to keep their thoughts and emotions much more private. They keep their distance mentally and physically. Controlling people place a high priority on getting things done and meeting deadlines. They like organization and structure and tend to make decisions based on facts.

By now you may be getting a pretty good idea of where you fall on these two scales and you may be asking yourself which is better—direct or indirect; supporting or controlling. There are no good or bad styles, they are just differences. The real question isn't which behavioral style is better, but how to best use the positive aspects of each trait while remembering that, taken to the extreme, each trait can be a drawback. We all face a variety of situations requiring different responses. What we want to do is learn when to use each behavior style.

If we put the two dimensions together, indirect to direct across, and supporting to controlling top to bottom, we get a four quadrant graph— what we call the Behavioral Style Grid and the four basic behavioral styles. While most people will display some traits of the other styles from time to time, a person's style describes how they behave most of the time.

To see a series of PowerPoint slides depicting the four quadrant grid, go to: http://www.alessandra.com/platinumruleslides

Dominant Directors

In the four-quadrant graph, the lower right quadrant is where direct and controlling overlap. We call the people who share those traits Dominant Directors. Dominant Directors are driven by an inner need to lead and be in personal control. They want to take charge of people and situations so they can reach their goals. Their key need is achieving so they seek no-nonsense, bottom-line results. Their motto is "Lead, follow, or get out of the way."

Directors want to win, so they often challenge people or rules. They accept challenges, take authority and plunge headfirst into solving problems. They tend to exhibit great administrative and operational skills and work quickly and impressively by themselves. They tend to be independent, strong-willed, precise, goal-oriented, cool and competitive with others, especially in a business environment. They try to shape their environment to overcome obstacles en route to their accomplishments. They demand maximum freedom to manage themselves and others, and use their leadership skills to become winners.

Their primary skills are their ability to get things done, lead others and make decisions. Directors have the ability to focus on one task to the exclusion of everything else.

Closely allied to their positive traits are the negative ones of stubbornness, impatience and toughness. Directors have a low tolerance for the feelings, attitudes and inadequacies of co-workers and subordinates.

Directors like to move at a fast pace and are impatient with delays. Directors tend to view others who move at a slower speed as incompetent.

Their weaknesses tend to be inflexibility, impatience, and poor listening habits and insensitivity to the needs of others. Their complete focus on their own goals and the task at hand can make them appear aloof and cool.

Directors are independent, strong-willed, precise, goal-oriented, cool and competitive. They accept challenges, take authority and expect others to do the same. They prefer to work with people who are decisive, efficient, receptive, and intelligent.

The competitive nature of the Director is probably typified by Vince Lombardi's statement that, "Winning isn't everything... it's the only thing!" Directors can be so single-minded that they forget to take the time to "smell the roses." And if they do remember, they may return and comment, "I smelled twelve roses today... how many did you smell?"

Cautious Thinkers

On our grid, the bottom left quadrant is where indirect and controlling overlaps in the Cautious Thinkers. Cautious Thinkers are detail-oriented, analytical, persistent, and systematic problem solvers. They are more concerned with content than style. Thinkers prefer involvement with products and services under specific, and preferably controlled, conditions so the performance, process, and results can be perfected.

The primary concern of the Cautious Thinker is accuracy. This often means that emotions take a back seat since they are subjective and tend to distort objectivity. Their biggest fear is of uncontrolled emotions and irrational acts that might prevent the achievement of their goals. Thinkers strive to avoid embarrassment by attempting to control both themselves and their emotions. They are very security-conscious and have a high need to be right, leading them to an over-reliance on the collection of data.

Thinkers prefer tasks to people and like to have clearly defined priorities. They like to operate at a steady pace that allows them to check and recheck their work. They tend to see the serious, more complicated sides of situations.

Thinkers demand a lot from themselves and others and may succumb to overly critical tendencies. Generally, they tend to keep their criticisms to themselves, hesitating to tell people what they think is deficient.

When Thinkers have definite knowledge of facts and details they quietly hold their ground. After determining the specific risks, margins of error, and other variables that significantly influence the desired results, they will take action.

Strengths of the Cautious Thinker include accuracy, dependability, independence, clarification and testing skills, follow-through and organization. They often focus on expectations such as policies, practices, and procedures and of course, outcomes.

Thinkers tend to be serious and orderly and are likely to be perfection-ists. They tend to focus on the details and the process of work and become irritated by surprises and glitches. They tend to be skeptical and like to see things in writing.

Because Thinkers need to be right, they prefer checking processes themselves. This tendency toward perfectionism, taken to an extreme, can result in "paralysis by overanalysis."

Thinkers can be seen as aloof, picky, and critical. Their fear of being wrong can make them over-reliant on the collection of data and slow to reach a decision. While Thinkers are good listeners and ask a lot of questions, they often focus too much on detail and miss the big picture.

Interacting Socializers

In the upper right corner of our grid, direct and supporting traits overlap to form the Interacting Socializers. They're friendly, enthusiastic and like to be where the action is. They thrive on admiration, acknowledgement, compliments and applause. They want to have fun and enjoy life. Energetic and fast-paced Socializers tend to place more priority on relationships than on tasks.

Often they're not as concerned about winning or losing as how they look while they're playing the game. The Socializer's greatest fear is public humiliation—they don't want to appear uninvolved, unattractive, unsuccessful or unacceptable to others. The Socializers' primary strengths are their enthusiasm, persuasiveness and friendliness. They are idea people who have the ability to get others caught up in their dreams. With great persuasion, they influence others and shape their environments by building alliances to accomplish their results.

Socializers are generally very open with their ideas and feelings. They are sometimes seen as "wearing their hearts on their sleeves." They are animated, interactive storytellers who have no qualms about "creative exaggeration." They love an audience and thrive on involvement with people. They tend to work quickly and enthusiastically with others.

Their weaknesses are too much involvement, impatience, aversion to being alone, and short attention spans. This causes them to become easily bored. When a little data comes in, Interacting Socializers tend to make sweeping generalizations. They may not check everything out, assuming someone else will do it, or may procrastinate because redoing something just isn't exciting enough.

When taken to an extreme, Socializer behaviors can be seen as superficial, haphazard, erratic and overly emotional. Their need for acknowledgement can lead to self-absorption. They have a casual approach to time and often drive the other styles crazy with their missed deadlines and lateness. The fun-loving, life-of-the-party Socializer can be undisciplined, forgetful, too talkative, and too eager for credit and recognition.

Steady Relaters

In the upper left corner of the Behavioral Grid, indirect and supporting traits overlap to form the Steady Relaters. The Steady Relaters are warm, supportive and reliable. They are the most people oriented of all of the four styles. Having close, friendly, personal, first name relationships with others is one of their most important objectives. They dislike interpersonal conflict so much that they sometimes say what they think other people want to hear. They have tremendous counseling skills and are extremely supportive. Relaters are excellent listeners and generally develop relationships with people who are also good listeners. As a result, they have strong networks of people who are willing to be mutually supportive.

Relaters focus on getting acquainted and building trust. They are irritated by pushy, aggressive behavior. They are cooperative, steady workers and excellent team players. They strive for security and try to maintain stability and a peaceful environment. While the unknown may be an intriguing concept, they prefer to stick with what they already know and have experienced. Risk is an ugly word to Relaters. They may even stay in an unpleasant environment rather than risk a change. Disruption in their routine patterns can cause them distress. If they are faced with a change, they need to think it through carefully and plan for the changes. Finding elements of sameness within those changes can help minimize their stress.

The primary strengths of Relaters are relating to, caring for, and loving others. They are courteous, friendly and willing to share responsibilities. They are good planners, persistent, and generally follow-through with their plans.

Relaters have difficulty speaking up and expressing their true feelings, especially if it might create conflict. They appear to go along with others even when they inwardly do not agree. They can be overly sensitive and easily bullied.

Their need for security makes them very slow at making decisions and this is often perceived as weakness or indecisiveness. In fact, their slowness results from their need to avoid risk and unknown situations and their desire to include others in the decision making process.

Identifying Your Prospects and Customers

Each of your customers will fall roughly into one of these four styles on the Behavioral Style Grid—Dominant Directors, Cautious Thinkers, Interacting Socializers, and Steady Relaters. In order to decide which style best describes your customer, you only need to make two decisions. Is your prospect more direct or indirect? More supporting or controlling?

By having to only make two decisions, you can quickly determine your customer's style. It's actually a process of elimination.

The first question is whether your customer is direct or indirect. Is she assertive, fast paced, makes swift decisions, takes risks, expresses opinions readily, impatient, and competitive? If so, she's more direct. However, if she's more easygoing, quiet, reserved, cooperative, asks and listens more than tells, avoids risks, and makes slower deliberate decisions, then she's indirect.

Ok, let's say that she is indirect. That means she is either a Thinker or a Relater, you've eliminated the direct styles of Socializer and Director. Now all you have to do is determine whether she is supporting or controlling.

Does she show her feelings openly, have a relationship priority, use more vocal inflection, have animated facial and body expressions, have a flexible time perspective, and make decisions more on emotions and feelings? If so, then she's more supporting. But, if she's more poker faced, keeps a distance physically and mentally, has a task priority, time disciplined, and makes decisions based more on logic and facts, she's more controlling. Let's assume that your observation says she is controlling —that eliminates the Relater, so she is a Cautious Thinker.

Developing a Relationship Strategy to Match Your Customer's Behavioral Style

Once you have determined your customer's style, you can start to treat your customer the way she wants to be treated. This often requires an adjustment in your behavior, specifically in your pace and priority. Since you can readily see whether the prospect is moving at a faster or slower pace than you, quickly make that adjustment. Then determine whether the prospect is focusing primarily on the relationship or the task and adjust accordingly.

Pace is the speed at which your customer prefers to operate. The direct styles (Socializers and Directors) prefer to move and decide quickly while the indirect styles (Relaters and Thinkers) prefer a slower, more cautious pace. If you go too fast for the indirect types, you will overrun their natural caution, but if you go too slowly for the direct types, you will irritate and frustrate them.

Priority is the second area where you'll need to adjust your behavior and it refers to whether the prospect wants to focus on the relationship or the task at hand. The Supporting styles (Relaters and Socializers) are relationship-oriented and will want to spend time getting to know you and letting you get to know them. The Controlling styles (Directors and Thinkers) will want to get down to the task immediately. Page 95 summarizes how you can effectively modify your pace and priority.

Here's an overview of specific strategies that works with each style:

With Dominant Directors—Be prepared, organized, fast-paced and always to the point. Meet them in a professional, business-like manner. Find out their goals and motivations. Get to the point quickly, provide options and let them make decisions when possible. To influence decisions, provide alternative actions with brief supporting analysis. If you disagree, argue facts—not personal feelings. Recognize their ideas—not them personally. Be punctual and don't waste their time. Above all else with the Director, be efficient and competent.

With Interacting Socializers—Show them that you are interested in them as a person. Support their opinions, ideas and dreams. Don't hurry the discussion. Try not to argue—you can seldom win. Let them talk and be enthusiastic and direct them toward mutually agreeable objectives. Provide testimonials and incentives to positively affect decisions. Summarize in writing the specifics of any agreement. Be entertaining and fast moving. Above all else with Socializers be interested in them.

With Steady Relaters—Get to know them personally. Be pleasant, friendly but professional and non-threatening. Develop trust and credibility at a relatively slow pace. Assume that they'll take everything personally. Ask them to explain their emotional needs as well as their task or business expectations. Get them involved by focusing on the human element. When you disagree, discuss personal feelings. Avoid rushing them and communicate with them on a consistent, regular basis. Show that you are actively listening. Provide guarantees and personal assurances that any actions will involve a minimum of risk. Above all else with the Relater, be warm and sincere.

With Cautious Thinkers—Be prepared and answer as many of their questions as soon as possible. Be systematic, exact and organized. Proceed quickly to the task. Demonstrate through actions rather than words. Explain your logic and ask questions that reveal a clear direction.

List advantages and disadvantages of any plan. Document how and why something applies. Provide solid, tangible and factual evidence. Give them time to think and avoid pushing them. Provide guarantees that actions can't backfire. Follow through and deliver what you promise. Above all else with the Thinker, be thorough and well prepared.

The key to success is to know whom you're dealing with and to be able to adapt to their needs. If you practice adjusting your selling style to fit the customer's buying style, you will create a situation where your customers are as eager to buy as you are to sell. At that point, you're ready to get into a serious exploration of their needs and concerns that we'll address in the next section.

STEP III

EXPLORING

▼

The Exploring stage of sales gives you a chance to get deeply involved with your prospect to determine exactly how your product or service can help him. It's where the partnering process begins.

The purpose of Exploring is to get enough information from the client to enable you to recommend appropriate options. But you have to do your homework first. Most salespeople do very little, if any, preparation before calling on the client. As a result, they ask poor questions that elicit minimal responses. Based on their incomplete picture of the client's situation, they make recommendations that may be totally inappropriate for the situation and then they can't understand why the client is reluctant to buy!

In this section we're going to show you how to prepare thoroughly for your meeting with the client, including what questions to ask and how to ask them. We'll show you how to actively listen to the client and take meaningful notes that you and the client can use together to solve the problem or take advantage of his opportunity. Then, we'll show you how to handle the actual in-person sales call. Some of what we'll cover will take you "back to the basics." You may have heard some of these ideas before... but it's important to use them effectively on every call.

CHAPTER 7

EXPLORING EFFECTIVELY
WITH QUESTIONS

▼

When we go into the field with salespeople from our client companies, we consistently find weakness in their ability to ask effective questions. We also find that they've been trained in this area but have not taken the time to apply what they've learned. We encourage you to make a commitment to master the skills included in the Explore stage of selling. They are the master skills of the successful salesperson and they will give you a lifetime Competitive Advantage.

Effective questioning requires good research and preparation to maximize its potential. There are lots of good sources of information. Any good library will have dozens of reference sources. For publicly held companies, you can locate their annual reports and get more information from Standard & Poor's Industry Survey. For smaller companies, check out Contacts Influential. And there are criss-cross directories and census reports for individual prospects. Your local business journal is also a good source of information and many brokerage firms now sell information on publicly traded companies. Also check with your local chamber and local and national associations for your target industries.

Make friends with the reference librarian at your local library. He can help you find out almost anything you want to know. Talk to people who use your prospect's product. Talk to his competitor's customers. After all, you're trying to help him be more competitive aren't you? Learn his industry so you can speak his language.

Develop a Questioning Plan

After you've researched your prospect, it's time to develop your questioning plan. You'll need to think through everything you need to know to fully understand your client's situation so you can make an appropriate, workable recommendation. Then develop a list of questions that will get you the information you'll need. That way you can concentrate on listening to your client's responses instead of trying to think up your next question.

In traditional selling, we were taught that the truly great salesperson went into the client's office like John Wayne and wrestled the client into submission with his bare hands. It was a display of raw power. Certainly, in that model of selling there was no room for thoughtful preparation... and there was no way John Wayne would ever show up with a list of questions! Are you kidding?

To bring you back to reality, put yourself in the customer's shoes. Imagine that you are thinking about remodeling your home. Being a smart consumer, you decide to have at least two contractors submit bids. The first one comes to your home, looks around your house, and asks you a few questions like, "How old is the house?" "What areas do you want to remodel?" "Will you need financing?" "How much equity do you have in the house?" "When do you want to start and when do you need it finished?" He then pulls out a contract, fills in several blanks, puts a price on it and asks you to sign on the bottom line.

Contractor #2 comes in with a sketchpad. On a separate pad he has a list of questions. His questions include: "Could you tell a little bit about what's prompting this project?" "In what area of your home do you spend the most time?" "What area of your home is your favorite and why?" "Which area is your least favorite and why?" As you discuss each area of your home, he takes detailed notes and then asks for a thorough tour. He sketches, measures and listens as you talk about your concerns and deadlines and before he leaves, he reviews his notes to make sure he hasn't forgotten anything. He asks you if it would be all right if he goes back to the office and prepares a plan, a schedule and a budget for your project. When you say yes, he requests a meeting with you in two days to discuss his ideas. Which contractor has your interest, your confidence, and your trust? On the basis of this first meeting, which contractor would you tend to hire?

Fact-finding versus Exploring

There are two big differences between the traditional contractor's method of fact-finding and the second contractor's method of exploring. One is the way the question is phrased and the other is the content of the response you are seeking. Fact-finding questions are typically closed-ended questions that can be answered with a yes, no or one word answer, while exploring questions are typically open-ended questions.

Examples of closed-ended questions include: "How long have you been in business?" or "How many bedrooms are you looking for in a home?" or "Are you happy with your current computers?" Examples of open-ended questions are: "Could you tell me a little about your company?" or "How would you describe your current personal investment strategy?" or "Tell me what's important to you in a home security system?"

The more significant difference between fact-finding and exploring is in the content of the response you are seeking. If your question only seeks to uncover raw data... facts, then it's a fact-finding question. While there's nothing wrong with those questions at the right time, they don't really give you much information about your prospect and his motivations.

On the other hand if you are trying to discover your customer's priorities, values, goals, ideas, view of the future, feelings, internal political concerns, financial situation, etc., then you are exploring!

Fact-finding questions that only seek raw data include: "How many computer workstations do you have now?" "How many people need to use them?" and "Do you own or lease?"

Exploring questions sound like this: "How do your people feel about your current workstation setup?" "What problems do they have getting access to a computer when they need one?" "What impact has the shortage had on productivity in your view?" and "What factors prompted your decision to own or lease?"

Fact-finding questions bore the client. Almost every computer salesperson asks those same questions... the prospect has probably heard them a dozen times. The minute you ask him this type of question, the prospect puts you into the "Just another Computer Salesperson" category and goes to sleep.

Whenever you work with a customer, you should always be looking for problems... and opportunities. The only two ways you can help your customer are to solve a problem for him or to help him take advantage of a new opportunity. Problems are things he wants to move away from and opportunities are the things he wants to move toward.

Most people have a dominant pattern of consistently moving away from problems or toward opportunities. If you can identify their pattern, you can position your product to meet their specific need by reflecting their language about the problem or opportunity. People who move away from problems are motivated primarily by a fear of something. These people tend to be the Thinkers and Relaters we profiled earlier. People who move toward opportunities are motivated primarily by a desire for something. These people tend to be the Directors and Socializers.

For instance, imagine that you're talking with an advertising agency about a new computer. The decision-maker says he would like to have a new computer but he can't buy one now because business is slow. You ask what he believes is causing the problem and he tells you he feels that he's lost touch with his clients. You ask what action he's taken and he says none. He's thought about several alternatives but rejected them all. His pattern is to move away. He is motivated by fear.

So you ask him if he's ever thought of doing a newsletter and he says, "Yes, but it seemed too complex and time consuming." His approach continues to be to "move away" from problems.

If, after you've finished exploring his situation, you could show him how he could move away from his problems of slow business and lost customer contact by using your computer's easy-to-learn, easy-to-use, problem-free desktop publishing system, you will have solved his problem of lost contact. If you can also show him how he can solve the cash flow problem with your easy payment plan that includes low monthly payments and no payment at all for the first 90 days, you will have solved his financing problem... and gotten a sale. You've also found out a lot about his business... and you've started to form a strong business relationship. You're not just trying to sell him something... you're trying to help him be more successful in his business.

Exploring questions challenge your customer to think more deeply about his situation and how it might be improved. They get him involved in the problem solving process and it's much more fun, creative work for your client than just responding with facts. Exploring is part of the process of building a relationship. You want to paint a complete picture of the customer's situation, not just the little corner that deals with his computer needs. You need to see your product in the context of his larger problem or opportunity. You want to find out his values and priorities... how he feels about the product or service. You're looking for a total solution not just a computer solution.

Many salespeople think that it's a waste of time to learn everything about a prospect's business when you only want to sell him a computer. They believe that you should just tell the prospect how great your computer is and ask for his order. That approach might be okay if you happened to walk in the day the prospect's current computer went dead. But, that's not normally the case. Usually, one of two things happens. Either you approach a prospect who is perfectly happy with his current computer system, or you approach a prospect who isn't happy with his current system and he's already talking to your competition.

If he's happy with his current computer, you'll need to ask some questions that start him thinking about its shortcomings or about the possibilities he's missing by not having state-of-the-art equipment. If he's not happy with his computer system but he's already talking to your competition, you'll need to know more about his situation, values, feelings and priorities than they do if you're going to come up with the most appropriate solution.

Recognize Your Customer's Priorities

One of the biggest reasons sales are lost is because of a poor understanding of the customer's priorities. How many times have you proposed the perfect solution to a significant problem only to have the customer tell you that while you did a great job, it just isn't a priority right now or that they just don't have the budget, or that the boss changed his mind? These are priority problems. Computers (or cars or overnight delivery or advertising services) may be important, maybe even critical, but if your customer has a higher priority... it's no sale. That's why understanding the complete picture is so important. It gives you the information you need to align your product or service within the customer's overall priorities.

If you ask a prospect only fact-finding questions, generally you'll quickly "discover" he's not interested... not a qualified prospect. You'll turn around, walk away and take his name off your prospect list. But, if you talk to him about his business and start to gather information about the problems he's facing... his challenges... you may uncover an opportunity. You might find out that he's losing sales by not having detailed information about inventory levels... something your whiz-bang computer will do easily for him. By finding out what his needs and expectations are, you let him know you are interested in him. You're beginning to build trust. In the end you may even find out he doesn't even need your computer. He might have the oldest, slowest computer in the world but it's meeting his needs perfectly. You may walk away without a sale, but you'll still have a relationship. And, someday, when that old, slow computer dies completely, the prospect will think of you because you were interested in him and his priorities.

Objections Are a Signal

Another signal that you need to do more exploring is when you find yourself getting a lot of objections at the end of your sales process. You get those objections because you're not doing enough exploring up front to truly understand your customer's situation. As you develop your list of questions, you'll need to think about the categories we'll list here plus whatever special information you'll need concerning your specific product.

The first topic to explore is Current situation: What is the prospect's current situation? Exactly what business is she in and where are the profits generated? Who are her customers? What are the problems and challenges facing her? What's happening in her industry? What's changing? What is the organization structure?

Next is desired situation: What would she like to have happen? Where would she like to see improvement? What would that improvement mean to her or her company? What are her goals and visions for his company? What are her personal goals? What concerns does she have about the future? What problems does she foresee?

After you've explored the customer's current situation and desired situation, you move on to Relevant past experiences: Has the customer had any recent experiences that have colored her thinking... maybe product failures, or personality conflicts, or service problems? These could also be exceptionally good experiences with other competitors that make her favor another vendor.

The difference between the current situation and the desired situation is the need gap. The smaller the need gap, the less likely any action will be taken by the prospect. The larger the need gap, the greater the desire to take immediate action to rectify—or close—it.

After analyzing a prospect's situation, if you find his need gap to be too small or nonexistent, then your product or service may offer little or no improvement. In this case, you would advise the client not to buy. When this happens, wrap up the call so you will not waste either your time or his. You might wrap things up by saying something like, "Mr. Jones, based on what we've discussed, it looks like I can't offer you a way to improve your sales. If, in the next six months, however, you find your sales do not grow by more than five percent (or some other condition), we would have a basis for doing business. Do you mind if I keep in touch to see how your sales are progressing?"

When you recontact him, ask how things are in general and then ask questions to see if those specific conditions have changed. If they have not, ask if you can call back again in three to six months. If they have changed, get together and look at his situation again.

Let's assume that the initial phase of exploration has yielded good results. The message is: "Let's continue talking." Now you'll need to explore the Decision making process: How does the decision making process work? How long is a normal decision process? Are there any deadlines involved?

Next, establish Decision criteria: What criteria will be used to determine the company and the product or service that is chosen? What are the customer's expectations? What is the relative value of each criterion?

Then, determine the Decision-makers: Simply ask, "Who, in addition to yourself, will be involved in the decision-making process?" Will the decision-makers consult any outside experts or authorities? Do some decision-makers carry more weight than others do—like the husband or the wife or the CPA? Does anyone have veto power? What role will each play?

In business-to-business sales, often the person who places the order isn't the person who makes the decision. So, when you interact with a company, it is essential to analyze the roles of the different people in the decision-making process. Some of these roles will overlap, but, for the most part, they will be divided into six types: We call them the Initiator, the Gatekeeper, the Influencer, the Decision-Maker, the Buyer and the User.

- the Initiator is the person who first suggests or thinks of buying a particular product or service.
- the Gatekeeper is a person, usually a secretary or receptionist, who has control over the accessibility of someone you wish to speak to or see.
- the Influencer is a member of the decision-making process whose opinion or advice is heavily weighed in the final decision.
- the Decision-Maker is obviously the person who is responsible for the ultimate decision of what to buy, how many, when and from whom.
- The Buyer is the person who actually makes the purchase, and
- the User is the consumer or person who is employing the product or service regularly.

In our computer example the roles might be as follows: the CFO would be the initiator, the accounting staff and service technicians would be the influencers, the CEO would be the decision maker, the head of purchasing would be the buyer, users would be the staffs of various departments, and several secretaries and receptionists would act as gatekeepers. Knowing how these roles impact the sales process can help you plan an effective strategy for winning the account.

In a complex situation like this, try to find an inside coach. As your ally, that person can guide you through the organization, provide you with key information and introduce you to other decision-makers.

And don't forget *politics:* Are there any hidden agendas that you need to know about? Do others in the organization or the household stand to gain or lose as a result of the final decision? Are there any special loyalties to other companies, other salespeople, or specific product brands? Politics or conflicts within an organization can often derail even a perfect sales plan. Asking about politics and agendas up-front can often reveal potential pitfalls and give you a chance to develop a strategy to handle them.

Let's consider the impact of negative past experiences: There are few sales situations as difficult as confronting a prospect who has a chip on his shoulder from a past injustice. The best thing to do is listen to the client and assure him you will do everything in your power to see that his bad experience is rectified and never repeated.

There's also competitive exposure to ask about: What other companies are being considered? Is the customer currently working with our competitors? What do they particularly like or dislike about the competition's offerings?

Be sure you establish success criteria and expectations: After the purchase, how will the client specifically measure the success of your product or service? Will this purchase impact his performance measurement process? Are there specific quality standards that must be met? The reason to ask these questions is to give you a concrete basis on which to measure the efficacy of your product or service after the sale. To accurately track performance, you need to have success criteria that are realistic, specific and measurable.

What is your customer's buying urgency? In exploring, it may be important for you to know how quickly a prospect will want to act if the sale were to be confirmed. The time factor gives you a lot of insight.

A prospect who recognizes a need but is in no hurry to change may be doing one of two things; either taking bids from competitors or gathering as much information as possible. It will be important for you to know which.

The urgency of the purchase will also impact your ability to deliver on promises. If there is some doubt as to the speed with which you can deliver, you will have to be a liaison between your prospect and your company. Go back to your company and see if you can convince them to rush the order if it comes through. This difficult balancing act is part of being a consultant representing the desires and limitations of two parties —the customer and the company. This is known as upstream and downstream selling. An example of this is seen in the insurance industry. An insurance salesperson has to sell you first and then go back to her company and sell underwriting on you being a safe bet to insure.

Finally, you must consider budget constraints: Is there a budget already committed to the project? How will the financial decision be made... return-on-investment? Payback period? Cost savings? Will financing be needed? "Who will provide it?"

All of these areas should be examined to create an exploration plan that makes sense for your prospect. Of course, this is a general guide and your prospect's unique situation may send you down an entirely different path. But by thinking through the situation in advance, you'll be prepared to be flexible. Preparation is a major part of Exploring and that it can yield big dividends when done well.

Once you've asked your clients the right questions, you need to know how to listen to the answers. The next chapter will give you a guide for listening not only to what your prospects say, but what they don't say. Active listening will give you the tools to make sense of all the information you've gathered from your prospects.

CHAPTER 8

ACTIVE LISTENING

▼

You've prepared a list of very important questions. Now it's important to focus on the specifics of how to be an effective listener. When we think of successful salespeople, we often think of a talker... someone who has a gift of gab... someone who's way with words convinces people to buy even if they aren't interested in the product or service. This talker-salesperson starts telling the prospect about his product before he even knows what the prospect needs or wants. That's what we refer to as prescription *before* diagnosis... and that's malpractice. Studies of the very best salespeople show that it's their listening skills that distinguish them from average performers... not their persuasive talking skills.

Ineffective listening is one of the most frequent causes of:
- misunderstandings
- mistakes
- jobs that need to redone
- lost sales and customers

If all of these negatives result from ineffective listening, why don't we listen more effectively? Here are several reasons:

Hard Work—Listening is more than just keeping quiet. An active listener registers increased blood pressure, a higher pulse rate, and more perspiration. It means concentrating on the other person rather than on ourselves. As a result, a lot of people just don't do it.

Information Overload—In today's society there is enormous competition for our attention from advertisements, radio, TV, movies, reading material, and more. With all this incoming stimuli, we have learned to screen out that information that we deem irrelevant. Sometimes we also screen out things that are important to us.

Rush to Action—We want to rush into action. We think we know what the person is going to say, so we jump in and interrupt, rather than taking the necessary time to listen and hear the person out.

Speed Difference—There is a considerable difference between speech speed and thought speed. The average person speaks at about 135 to 175 words a minute, but can listen to 400 to 500 words a minute. So, the poor listener spends all that time between the speed with which he listens and the speed with which he talks, on daydreams . . . or on thoughts of what he is going to say next . . . or in mentally arguing with the person speaking. It's like listening to two voices at the same time.

Lack of Training—We do more listening than speaking, reading, or writing, yet we receive almost no formal education in listening. In fact, the average student gets less than one-half year of listening education through her first 12 years of schooling!

Listening well—listening actively—is obviously important, but how does it really benefit you? Listening well has the following benefits:
- Improves the environment at work, at home, and in sales.
- Reduces relationship tensions and hostilities.
- Saves time by reducing mistakes and misunderstandings.
- Leads to early problem solving.
- Increases sales and profits.

Let's start by defining listening as the process of receiving a message the way the customer intended to send it. Remember that an untrained listener misses as much as 50% of the message and reflect on how that could affect the sales process. Every time a customer says, "I didn't understand," or "Is that what you meant?" or "I didn't hear you say that," or "We had a misunderstanding due to poor communication," it's because the salesperson didn't practice good listening skills.

There are three levels of listening: *marginal listening,* evaluative listening and active listening. The lowest level of listening—marginal listening—involves the least concentration. Surroundings, and his own thoughts, distract the salesperson. You'll probably recognize this state by the person's blank stares or nervous mannerisms. Any salesperson who's listening at this level is in deep trouble. The prospect will feel your lack of attention, be insulted and lose trust in you. For example, a prospect looking at a copy machine might say, "I'm not sure it's big enough to handle my needs." The marginal listening salesperson responds, "We offer a three year warranty with each machine." The salesperson is running through a spiel and not connecting with the information the customer is offering.

At the next level of listening—evaluative listening—the salesperson is paying attention and concentrating somewhat. The salesperson is hearing the words but not the intent. In evaluative listening, the salesperson leaps ahead to what he thinks the message is going to be and prepares an answer before the customer is even finished with his statement. When the customer states the concern about the size of the copy machine, the *evaluative listening* salesperson would hear the concern about size and leap to a canned response... "We have copiers that can handle any copy volume." He makes an assumption about the customer's concern and responds in a way that may not be appropriate. Neither marginal listening nor evaluative listening is sufficient for a competitive advantage.

The third and most effective level of listening is active listening. The active listener refrains from evaluating the message and tries to see the prospect's point of view. Attention is not only on the words spoken but also on the thoughts and ideas... on the intent. When our copying machine prospect makes the statement about it being big enough to meet her needs, the *active listening* salesperson says, "Tell me more about what you need in a copy machine."

The salesperson defers his judgment *and the sales presentation* until he knows more about the customer needs. He is trying to get past the words to find out the real concern behind the prospect's statement. Behind the words are a lot of thoughts and feelings... our prospect may be concerned about the copier capacity, or she may be concerned about speed. She may also just be talking about physical size and wondering if it will fit in the space she has in mind for it!

Active listeners listen *behind* the words for the *thoughts and feelings* but they also listen *between* the words for what is *not* being said. Sometimes customers reveal much more by what they don't say. There are several ways to hear the emotions behind the words. First, look for changes in eye contact. After you have established a comfortable and natural level of eye contact, any sudden deviations from the norm will tip you off to emotional content in the message. People tend to look away from you when they talk about something embarrassing. When this happens, make a quick mental note of what subject caused the embarrassment and treat that subject delicately. You should also give your prospect the courtesy of looking away momentarily yourself, as if you are saying, "I respect your privacy."

These five steps, when followed, will help you become an active listener:

1. Concentrate by focusing your attention on the customer and only on the customer.
2. Acknowledge your customer by demonstrating your interest and attention.
3. Research gathering information about your customer through the skillful use of questions and statements.
4. Sense the nonverbal messages of your customer by observing what he's saying with his body language.
5. Structure, or organize, the information you get through your listening, observation and note taking.

How Do Your Listening Skills Rate?

Before you begin working to improve your listening skills, let's first look at where you are at this moment in each of the key areas of effective listening. Take a few minutes to respond to the questions below. Your responses will help you determine what specific skills need improvement. Respond honestly to each of the items—no one is going to review or use this survey but you.

Concentrate

1. When I talk with others, my mind is completely absorbed by what they are saying and it seldom wanders.
   ❑ Always   ❑ Sometimes   ❑ Never
2. When in a conversation with others, I hold my comments until they are finished talking, even though my comments may have direct relevance to what they are saying at that moment.
   ❑ Always   ❑ Sometimes   ❑ Never
3. I do not let distractions like ringing telephones, busy street traffic, or other conversations in a room distract my attention from what someone is saying to me.
   ❑ Always   ❑ Sometimes   ❑ Never

Acknowledge

4. When talking face-to-face or on the phone with someone, I acknowledge what is being said with "I understand" or "I see" or other comments that let's the customer know I'm listening to him.
   ❑ Always   ❑ Sometimes   ❑ Never

Research

5. Whenever I talk with someone, I encourage the conversation and ensure that it will be a two-way flow of communication by asking open-ended questions, clarifying what I don't completely understand, and giving appropriate feedback.
   ❑ Always   ❑ Sometimes   ❑ Never

6. I let others know that I am listening and trying to understand what they say by using phrases like, "Tell me more about that," or, "Can you give me an example?" or "Then what?"
   ❑ Always   ❑ Sometimes   ❑ Never

Sensing

7. When I am talking with others, I read their body language, as well as listen to their words, to fully interpret what they are telling me.
   ❑ Always   ❑ Sometimes   ❑ Never

8. When talking with others, I try to read what's going on behind their spoken words by asking myself what they might be feeling, why they are saying what they are saying, and what is implied by what they say.
   ❑ Always   ❑ Sometimes   ❑ Never

Structure

9. Whenever I talk with others, I either take mental or written notes of the major idea, the key points, and the supporting points and/or reasons.
   ❑ Always   ❑ Sometimes   ❑ Never

10. As I take my mental or written notes, I sequence—I listen for order or priority.
    ❑ Always   ❑ Sometimes   ❑ Never

Now that you have responded to the items above, you have a road map for improving your listening skills. Any item marked as "Sometimes" or "Never" identifies a listening skill that needs improvement. For any item marked as "Always"—*Congratulations!*

Now let's talk about the specifics of how to be a better active listener. The first technique is Concentrate—clear the distractions around you whenever possible—ringing telephones, high noise levels, and interruptions. You also need to clear your internal distractions—concerns about your family or upcoming deadlines... anything that might keep you from devoting 100% of your attention to the customer. All of those worries or distractions will still be waiting for you once you're finished with the customer. It is also important not to interrupt the customer or try to rush him.

To become an active listener, then, you must *concentrate* completely on the customer. As the salesperson, you must eliminate as many distractions as possible when listening to others. All distractions create enormous barriers that prevent the message from getting from the customer to you, the listener.

Here are some ways you can concentrate better on the customer

Create a receptive listening environment. Such an environment is a place that is as devoid as possible of any audio or visual distractions. Try to have a private, quiet, comfortable setting, especially in terms of temperature and seating. If you're meeting at the customer's place of business, you have less control over the external environment, but if there are a lot of distractions, such as phones ringing or frequent interruptions, you can recommend moving into a meeting room with more privacy. If that's not possible, suggest a later meeting in a more receptive listening environment on neutral territory such as a quiet out-of-the-way restaurant.

Avoid violating another person's personal space. Some people are "contact-oriented" while others are "non-contact" oriented. When you're talking with people, keep in mind that some may be very open and like to communicate in close proximity, while others may tend to be more self-contained and want to keep a greater physical distance.

Contact-oriented people tend to sit much closer to those with whom they are speaking. They communicate much closer as well and they even touch when they communicate. Some cultural backgrounds in which this is quite common are Italian, Arab, Greek, several of the Mediterranean cultures, French, and the Latin American cultures. Examples of non-contact cultures would include the Japanese, the German, the English and to some degree the American.

Focus—When distractions can't be avoided, minimize them by totally focusing and concentrating on the customer. Use the following four techniques of applied concentration to help you focus and concentrate on the customer:

Mentally paraphrase what the customer is saying. Mentally paraphrasing what the customer is saying will prevent you from daydreaming or thinking of irrelevant and superfluous topics, especially if the customer to whom you are listening speaks slowly. Try to echo, rephrase, evaluate, anticipate, and review what the customer is saying so that you focus and concentrate on the customer instead of yourself.

Visually observe the other person. Keep in mind the Hitchhiking Theory: where your eyes focus, your ears will follow. You are most likely to listen to what you are looking at. Make direct eye contact for several seconds before looking away. Prolonged eye contact may convey either intimidation or intimacy.

Concentrating *completely* on the person speaking to you requires these two steps:

* Eliminate, or at least diminish, all distractions.
* Focus your attention solely and directly on the person speaking.

In the context of active listening, acknowledging means that salespeople give positive, observable, and frequently audible signs to the customer that they are listening to, understanding, and appreciating what the customer says. As an active listener, your acknowledgment communicates an attitude of acceptance of the customer as a worthwhile person. On the other hand, non-acknowledging or negative acknowledging demonstrated by the poor listener communicates disapproval and rejection, and weakens the relationship between the customer and the salesperson. The result of such poor acknowledging is an interruption or an end of the communication process.

Think again of that person with whom you enjoy sharing conversations. In the lists below, which group contains the words that describe the body language and gestures of the person who shows an interest in you and what you are saying?

Glances sideways.	Looks in your eyes.
Sighs.	Touches your arm or hand.
Crosses arms on chest.	Leans toward you.
Leans away from you.	Smiles frequently.
Stares.	Maintains a pleasant facial expression.
Sneers.	Grins.
Yawns.	Sits so as to face you directly.
Frowns.	Nods head affirmatively as you speak.
Looks at the ceiling.	Licks lips.
Shakes head negatively.	Raises eyebrows.
Cleans fingernails.	Keeps eyes wide open.
Cracks knuckles.	Uses expressive hand gestures while speaking.
Jingles change or rattles keys.	Gives fast glances.
Fidgets in chair.	Stretches.

The gestures on the first list usually make us feel like someone isn't very interested in what we're saying while the second list contains many of the gestures people use to let us know they're listening. In addition to the non-verbal acknowledgment, an active listener acknowledges the customer verbally as well with such comments as, "I see," "Uh-huh," "Then what?" "Mmmm," or "Really?" Even the empathic comments such as, "I don't believe it!" show the customer that you're alert, you're listening and that you care.

When acknowledging your customer both verbally and non-verbally, you accomplish many things that build trust and increase the customer's comfort level. Through your acknowledgment, the customer knows that you:

- Are *listening*.
- Understand the *content* of what is being said.
- Understand how he/she *feels*.
- Understand the essential *meaning* of what is being said.
- Are *interested* in him/her and what is said.

As an *active* listener, researching is what you do to keep a conversation a two-way communication. It's the information-gathering techniques of questioning and feedback. It enables you to clarify what you've heard, enlarge upon a subject or go into a particular topic in more depth. Researching allows you to encourage the customer to change the direction of the conversation or to prompt the customer to "vent" such feelings as anger, excitement, and enthusiasm. It also allows you to support and reinforce particular parts that one has said to you.

The person who doesn't *actively* participate in the conversation through questions and feedback will make the customer feel uncomfortable by creating an information imbalance. Such an information imbalance occurs when one person does all the talking and provides all the information while the other person simply listens—or *appears* to listen. Eventually the customer becomes concerned that the salesperson knows a lot about him but he doesn't know *anything* about the salesperson. Such a situation can make the customer feel tense and suspicious.

Your ability to ask the right questions at the right time while responding with appropriate *feedback* is essential and integral parts of the skill of researching. We already covered the art of asking questions, so let's focus more on the effective use of feedback.

Feedback

Feedback is the other important aspect of researching if conversation is to continue for any length of time. Without giving feedback, how does the salesperson "really" know what the customer is trying to communicate? The effective use of feedback helps ensure that you will receive an accurate message.

You use feedback whenever you react verbally, vocally or visibly to what another person says or does. Listening *actively* depends on it.

As a listener, you give feedback in several ways. You give verbal feedback, nonverbal feedback (as we discussed in the acknowledge section) and feeling feedback. Each serves a specific purpose in active listening.

Verbal Feedback

Verbal feedback is what you use most often. You use it to give and to ask for clarification of what the customer said and you use it to encourage the customer to continue. In clarifying that you understood what was said, reflect back to the customer your understanding of what was said. Note that we said, "reflect back . . ." rather than *"repeat* back." In other words, be sure that you use *your own words;* otherwise you will simply be parroting the customer's words instead of demonstrating your understanding of what was said. Example:

Customer: The last copier I bought was always down or having to be serviced.

Salesperson: (Parroting) The last copier you bought had a lot of service problems.

Salesperson: (Verbal Feedback) You seem to be afraid that a new copier might have lots of down time and service problems.

As for clarifying to improve your understanding of what was said, you can use such phrases as:

I get the impression that you feel...

I sense that...

It sounds like you...

In other words,...

What I'm hearing is...

Be sure to vary your introductory words when clarifying what has been said, otherwise it will appear as though you're really not listening but simply following a script.

Verbal feedback can also take the form of broad questions and the appropriate follow-up questions built on the customer's responses that were discussed earlier.

Nonverbal Feedback

Projecting positive nonverbal feedback to the customer through gestures and utterances lets the customer know that her message is getting through to you. People want feedback—they need feedback. They don't like to talk with people who don't respond or show any emotion.

Feeling Feedback

Obviously a firm understanding of the words, phrases, and facts of a message is important. However, that still represents just surface understanding. Why is the person saying the things she is saying? What are the underlying causes and motivations behind her message? How does she really feel about what she is saying to you? Does she know whether her message is really getting through to you—at the feeling level? Is she aware that you really care about what she is saying to you?

All these questions underscore the importance of *feeling* feedback in active listening. Feeling feedback should be two-directional. You need to make a concerted effort *to understand* the feelings, emotions, and attitudes that underlie the message that comes to you. In addition, you should clearly *project feeling feedback* to the other person to demonstrate that her message has gotten through to you—at the feeling level.

Feeling feedback is a meeting of the hearts. It is nothing more than the effective use of empathy—putting yourself into the other person's shoes so that you can see things from his point of view. When you can really experience the other person's true feelings and understand where she's coming from and at the same time project this emotional awareness to her, it serves to reinforce rapport, lower interpersonal tension, and significantly increase trust. Supportive and understanding responses and an awareness and projection of appropriate nonverbal signals are the key tools used in sending and receiving feeling feedback.

When listening to someone, try to read the primary feeling the customer is projecting and respond to that feeling, allowing then for the customer to agree or to correct your "reading." For example:

Salesperson: You seem to be somewhat distressed about the service you've received.

Customer: Somewhat distressed? Are you kidding? I'm very angry about the mismanagement of the entire situation!

Another technique that is excellent for getting people to respond and share their feelings and thoughts with you is the use of empathy statements. Empathy statements consist of three specific parts:

- a tentative statement;
- defining the feeling;
- putting the feeling into its situational context.

An example of such an empathy statement is:

"It seems to me that you're very frustrated because you can't get the product to work the way you want it to work."

The phrase, "It seems to me," is the tentative statement. The phrase, "you're very frustrated," defines the feeling, and the phrase, "because you can't get the product to work the way you want it to work," is putting the feeling into its situational context—the situation that caused the customer to experience the feeling of frustration.

Sensing refers to the ability to perceive messages sent *vocally* and *visually* as well as verbally. We respond to the gestures of others based on a preconscious understanding of the "secret" code of nonverbal communication—the *vocal* and *visual* messages sent by those speaking.

Body Language

The concept of body language—the visual part of nonverbal communication—is certainly not new. People have known about it and have used it since the beginning of time. Before people developed language as a communication tool, they used body language to make their needs and desires known to others. Also known as kinesics, body language describes human interaction beyond the use of written and spoken words.

Some nonverbal gestures represent universal symbolism. The chair at the head of the table has long been reserved for the leader of the group. More recently, this position of honor has also been extended to the host of the table. Another universal gesture is raising the hands above the head, which has long symbolized surrender and submission.

Some gestures are even more expressive than words. Conjure up the image of a person slapping his forehead. This may be accompanied by an audible groan. Don't you already know that he has remembered something he was supposed to do? Implicit in this gesture is a rebuke to himself for his oversight. Other well-known gestures are saluting, tipping one's hat, shaking hands, shrugging shoulders, waving good-bye, forming an "O" with thumb and forefinger, and blowing a kiss.

Body language involves the salesperson's interpretation of many kinds of gestures made by the customer's eyes, face, hands, arms, legs, and posture of the customer. You can glean a considerable amount of information about others and them about you, simply by noting body gestures. However, each isolated gesture is like an isolated word in a sentence—it is very difficult and dangerous to interpret the gesture by itself or out of context. Unless it's a one-word sentence, it takes more than one gesture to provide full meaning. Consequently, you should consider the gesture in light of everything else that's going on around you.

Interpreting gesture clusters ensures a more meaningful analysis of the customer's state of mind, if they are in harmony with the other messages being sent by the customer. In other words, all the individual gestures must fit together to project a common, unified message. When they do not, you are faced with incongruity. A good example of incongruity is a nervous laugh. Remember that body language can augment, emphasize, or even contradict the words that someone is speaking.

Let's examine some of the more common gesture clusters and their associated meanings.

Openness: Several gestures indicate openness and sincerity, such as open hands, unbuttoned coat or unbuttoned collar, the removing of a coat or jacket, moving closer together, leaning slightly forward in the chair, and uncrossed arms and legs.

Defensiveness: On the other hand, defensiveness is usually projected by a rigid body, rigid or tightly crossed arms or legs, eyes glancing sideways or darting occasionally, minimal eye contact, lips pursed, fists clenched, and downcast head. Be especially aware of tightly clenched fists—they show that the other person is really turned off. Evaluation: Evaluation gestures suggest that the other person is considering what you are saying, sometimes in a friendly way—sometimes unfriendly. Typical evaluation gestures include the tilted head, the hand to cheek, leaning forward, and chin stroking. Sometimes evaluation gestures take on a critical aspect. In this case, the body is usually more drawn back, the hand is to the face, but the chin is in the palm of the hand with one finger going up the cheek and the other fingers positioned below the mouth.

Self-conflict: This is usually expressed by a person pinching the bridge of his nose or closing his eyes, and slumping his head down slightly. He is probably trying to decide if he's in a bad situation or not. Don't try to reason him out of it, give him time.

Negative Evaluation: A person dropping his eyeglasses to the lower bridge of the nose and peering over them is projecting a negative evaluation. Suspicion, secrecy, rejection, and doubt are communicated typically by sideways glances, minimal or no eye contact, shifting the body away from the customer, and touching or rubbing the bridge of the nose quite frequently.

Readiness: This is another cluster that communicates dedication to a goal. It's usually communicated by placing the hands on the hips or sitting forward at the edge of a chair.

Boredom or Impatience: These are usually conveyed by the drumming of fingers, cupping the head in the palm of the hand, foot-swinging, brushing or picking at lint, doodling, pointing the body toward an exit, or looking at your watch or looking at the exit.

In addition to observing gesture clusters, be watchful for changes in the gestures themselves which can indicate important changes in attitudes. For example:

Positive Change <———>	Negative Change
Relaxing	Tensing
Increased eye contact	Decreased eye contact
Leaning forward	Leaning away
Uncrossing arms, legs	Crossing arms, legs
Matching body position and gestures with customer's	Fidgeting
Smiling	Frowning

Vocal Intonation

Your total reception of a customer's message depends not only the verbal and visual aspects of communication, but also on what you hear *behind* the words—the *vocal* part of the message heard through voice intonations.

People can project many different emotions simply through their voice intonation. Voice intonation gives the vocal information; the words spoken give the verbal information. Vocal information is that part of the meaning of a message that is lost when speech is written rather than spoken. Added meaning can be derived from the words others speak and additional meaning can be added to the words you speak simply by changing voice intonation.

Let's take a look at the seven major vocal qualities that affect voice intonations:

Resonance: The ability of one's voice to fill space, an intensification and enrichment of the voice tone

Rhythm: The flow, pace, and movement of the voice

Speed: How fast or slow the voice is used

Pitch: The tightening or relaxing of the vocal cords—for example, the nervous laugh—and the highness or the lowness of sound

Volume: The degree of loudness or intensity of the voice

Inflection: The changes in pitch or volume of the voice

Clarity: The crisp articulation and enunciation of the words

The way in which a person varies any or all of these seven vocal qualities in conversation can significantly change the feeling or emotion of the message being sent. A good example of what changes in meaning can result from changes in voice qualities is an actor who verbalizes the word "oh" eight different ways:

"Oh!" (Exclamation—"Oh! I forgot to mail the check!")

"Oh!" (Excitement—"Oh! Wow!")

"Oh?" (Question—"Oh? Is that right?")

"Oh" (Passion—"Oh... I love opera.")

"Oh" (Disgust—"Oh, not peas again!")

"Oh" (Pain—"Oh, my arm hurts.")

"Oh" (Disbelief—"Oh, yeah?")

"Oh" (Boredom—"Oh. How interesting.")

With just simple changes in vocal qualities, a customer can convey eight totally separate and unique feelings and emotions to the salesperson. This simple two-letter word—"Oh"—demonstrates the critical importance of vocal intonation in communication.

In summary, Sensing is hearing spoken messages through vocal and visual channels. Sensing in a very real sense is like learning another language—learning to "speak," use, and understand *body* talk. As Ralph Waldo Emerson said, *"What you ARE is shouting so loud, I can't hear what you are saying."*

Structuring is listening primarily to the verbal component—the content—of someone's message. The structuring process revolves around three primary activities—indexing, sequencing and comparing.

Indexing refers to taking mental or written notes of:

1. The topic or major idea;
2. The key points being discussed;
3. The reasons, sub-points, and/or supporting points.

This process is made easier by listening for transitional words. Transitional words are words and phrases like, "Well, what I want to talk to you about today is... ." What follows such phrases is probably the main idea, the subject, or the topic. Also, "first," "second," "third," and "last" are transitional words that usually indicate key points. When people say things like, "For example," or "Let me elaborate on that," you know that a rationale, a sub-point, or a supporting point is likely to follow.

Since we can listen much faster than a person can talk, we can use that time to take notes and make sense of what is being said. You may need to ask permission to take notes and do it as unobtrusively as possible. You don't need to take verbatim notes... just get the highlights down to jog your memory later. Taking notes also helps you to focus your attention completely on what your customer is saying.

You have to be able to gather an incredible amount of information, make sense of it and find a solution to his problems or a way to help him meet his goals... hopefully through using your product or service. In order to gather and organize all that information, you can use an advanced note-taking technique called mindmapping that also helps you find creative solutions to the customer's problems. This technique helps you take notes quickly without breaking the flow of the conversation and helps you to create on paper a visual of what your customer is saying. It is a superior method of note taking in three important ways.

1. It increases the speed with which you can structure and organize the content of what you hear.
2. It increases your comprehension and retention of what you hear when you refer to your notes after the conversation.
3. It motivates you to keep pace with the customer.

Mindmapping sounds complex, but it's actually quite simple. Mindmapping is a visual form of note taking and it can help get your client involved with the process of information gathering. It also helps him appreciate your efforts to make sense of his situation and help him find solutions. Because it looks different from most note taking systems, it also helps differentiate you from your competition. Because we can think four times as fast as a customer can talk, our thoughts often race ahead of the customer, and we detach from what is being said. Through mindmapping, you can easily remain focused on the customer. It's extremely easy to use. Here are the basics:

- Focus—Print the central or main idea in a circle or box in the center of your page for notes.
- Branches—Write the key ideas or thoughts expressed on lines (branches) connected to the center focus.
- Twigs—Draw sub-branches or twigs—one for each related idea expressed, and connect the twigs to the key idea each supports.
- Key Words—Write key words only. Mindmapping is a form of brain shorthand and requires only key words to jog your memory.
- Symbols/Images—Use any symbols or images that make sense to you. Make use of arrows, pictures, other symbols meaningful to you—whatever jogs your memory and doesn't take your mind from what you're hearing.

Mindmapping is fun, it doesn't intrude on your concentration, and it captures the essence of what you are listening for. There are two ways to use mindmapping with your customers. You can just develop a mindmap informally as you ask the customer questions or you can actually prepare in advance a mindmap of the information you want to gather from the customer. This could be on a notepad... something big enough to write on that can be seen easily by both you and the client, but small enough to fit into your briefcase. You would start out with your client's name in the center of the page and then have branches off of that for the information you would want to gather.

The branches of your mindmap would match the topic areas in your list of questions. As you work through the mindmap with your client you'll both have a visual feedback tool that will help you to get a complete picture of your customers' needs. You also have a guide that reminds you of what information you want to gather. You can make any specific notes you want on the branches. For instance, if you knew your customer's industry was facing a potentially devastating series of government regulations, you could have a line off the "Challenges" branch that said, "Govt. regs." This would remind you to ask how those regulations would impact him. Or if the prospect is in the highest tax bracket, you could devote a branch to that to explore how it might affect his estate planning or pension needs. Here is an example of a mind-map:

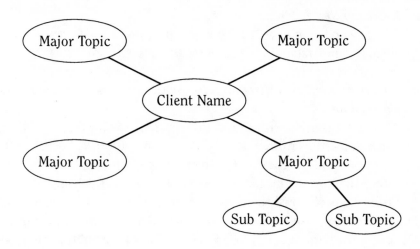

One of the things mindmapping does is give both of you an overview of the situation. It keeps you from getting bogged down in details. And it also encourages your customer to complete the picture. The visual representation of his situation will prompts him to keep filling in the blanks until the mindmap is complete. It gets the customer involved. It also keeps you involved, so it helps you become a better active listener. There are books to help you develop your skill with mindmapping. Check out *Mindmapping: Your Personal Guide to Creativity and Problem-Solving* by Joyce Wycoff or books by Tony Buzan.

The Power of Listening

You have now learned each step of active listening. The skills are now yours to use . . . or are they? Although these skills are all relatively simple to learn and may appear simple to use, *implementing* them may be a more difficult task, because to do so means breaking through a barrier of poor listening habits that most of us have developed over a lifetime.

Creating and exercising an active listening *attitude* can help you tremendously in breaking through the barrier of your poor listening habits and implementing your newly acquired active listening skills. Exercising an Active Listening Attitude means:

1. *Understanding that listening is as powerful as speech.*
   What people say to you is just as critical as what you have to say to them.
2. *Realizing that listening saves time.*
   People who listen find that it creates fewer mistakes, fewer interpersonal misunderstandings, less employee and customer turnover and fewer false starts.
3. *Understanding that listening to EVERYONE is important and worthwhile.*
   Approach listening with a new enthusiasm. Look for that something you can learn from each and every person you meet. Focus on the substance and the meaning of the message that people are sending rather than on the mechanics or the style of their delivery.

Listening is obviously a critical part of the Exploring stage of sales. One of the things we hear salespeople say frequently is, "Opening the sales call is the hardest part. I'm O.K. once I get rolling but those first few minutes are pretty rough. I'm never quite sure what to say." By practicing active listening skills you make the opening easy. You don't have to worry about what to say or how to say it; you just have to ask questions, listen actively, and follow the direction of the prospect. As you follow the prospect's lead, it is important to stay in sync with him. The next chapter will give you several ideas and techniques for making a powerful connection with your prospects and customers.

CHAPTER 9

EXPLORING NEEDS
AND OPPORTUNITIES

▼

The most important thing to focus on in the first few minutes of a sales call is getting in sync with the customer. As much as possible you want to match his attitude, his demeanor and his business values. Concentrate on his pace. If it is faster or slower than yours... adjust yours. If he is focusing on the task, then get right to business. If he is focusing on the relationship, then take a few minutes to chat. In the first few moments let the client lead and you follow. Wait until the two of you are in sync... then you can try to lead the discussion.

Use your competitive advantage statement early in the call. Remember, your competitive advantage statement should have four components... your name... your company... a statement about a problem in your market... and how you and your product can solve that problem. After all, it was the use of this competitive advantage statement on the phone that got you the appointment so there must be some interest. Restating your competitive advantage helps to refresh your prospect's memory and get the customer grounded in the discussion you are about to have. If he's being task oriented, use it right up front. If he's being relationship oriented, chat for a few moments, and then use your positioning statement as a transition from relationship to task behavior. "Thank you for the coffee. As I mentioned on the phone..."

The most powerful aspect of synchronization is values. If he believes you share his values, he's very likely to want to do business with you now or sometime in the future. So, how do you let the customer know your values are in sync with his? You want to let him know that you are a professional and that you're not just there to make a sale. You want to say something like this:

"My approach to doing business is to partner with you. I am an expert in the products, services and processes that my company offers but they will be no good to you unless they fit in your environment. You're the expert in those areas. For us to be effective partners we have to share our expertise in collaboration. I'll make you four promises... First, I promise you I'll provide you with fast, high quality information in my area of expertise. Second... I'll never pressure you to make a decision or to buy anything from me. Third, you have no obligation to buy from me, no matter how much time and effort we spend trying to find solutions. And fourth, I promise not to waste your time. If I don't feel that I can help you, I'll tell you so. You will be in total control of the process.

In return for my promises, I ask two things of you... total honesty even when it's something I may not want to hear, and your total participation in the process of exploring your needs and collaborating on possible solutions.

If you'll collaborate with me, you'll get a free consultant and all the credit for the solutions we identify. I may or may not get an order. The reason I can afford to work with you like this is because you match the profile of my best customers and I want you as a lifetime customer if it's appropriate.

So, once the customer agrees to go along with your "partnering" approach to the sales process, what do you do next? You actually begin exploring the customer's needs and expectations, problems and opportunities, by using your questioning and listening skills. Asking questions is similar to painting a picture. We start with a blank canvas and begin to fill in the background and rough in the picture with broad-brush strokes. Then we fill in the details using finer and finer strokes.

Funnel Technique of Questioning

With questioning, we start with broad strokes asking the customer exploring, open-ended questions that fill in a lot about his situation. "Could you tell me a little bit about your business," or "Could you tell me what's important to you in choosing a financial institution?" not only starts to give you information about your prospect's situation, they give him a chance to relax and tell you what he thinks is important. Open-ended questions do not lead the customer in a specific direction. They increase dialogue by drawing out the customer. If you start with a fact-finding question, such as "How much can you afford to spend on a home?"—that's an okay question, but affordability may not be your prospect's primary concern right now.

Exploratory, open-ended questions show your interest in the prospect's situation. They often start with "Tell me," "how," "who," "what," or "why." "How do you see a new computer system fitting into your current operation?" "What would you like your new cellular phone to do for you?" "What prompted you to look for a new travel agency right now?" They are much more powerful than closed-ended, fact-finding questions that require a simple answer such as yes or no or a specific piece of information.

Of course, we will use closed questions when we need specific answers such as "How many members of your family will be using the new stereo system?" Closed-ended questions are used to extract simple and specific facts or to direct the conversation in specific directions. But, it's important to understand when to use each type of question. Once you've started the questioning process, you want to build on whatever responses you've gotten. You are following the lead of your prospect.

We call this the *Funnel Technique* of questioning—you start with broad, open questions such as "Could you tell me a little bit about your long-term financial goals?" You build on his response by then asking narrower and more specific questions. As you move down the funnel, you paint with a finer brush and fill in the details. Graphically, it would look something like this:

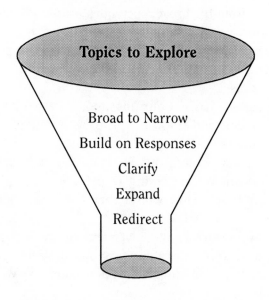

Assume your prospect responds to your question about why he wants a computer system with, "I need more control over our order system." You build on his response by building a question around the operative word in his answer. For instance you might respond with "What aspects of your order system would you like to have more control over?" "What's happening that's making you feel out of control, now?" or "Could you tell me more about your order system?" When he responds, you'll build your next question around his response to that question and so on until you feel you've got a good understanding in that area and then you'll move on to a different area of your mindmap and begin again with a broad open exploring question in that area.

The broad, open questions at the top of the funnel are comfortable for the customer to answer. They give him the freedom to tell you whatever he wants. By the time you get to the more specific questions, the customer can see where you're going and he's more willing to share information with you. Not only that, most people experience a higher sense of trust and willingness to share information proportionately to how much information they have previously shared. Their willingness tends to increase at an increasing rate as they provide more information to you. So knowing how to open your prospect up with comfortable, broad, open questions at the outset of the meeting becomes a significant competitive advantage.

As you move from the broad, open questions to the narrower, more specific questions, you'll develop a clearer idea of what the prospect's primary concerns and needs are. At the end of the process, you'll probably need to ask more closed-ended questions to get the specific information you need.

Questions are the basis of our information gathering activities but it's helpful to understand the three primary directions for questions; expand, clarify and redirect.

When we want more information about a certain area, we ask an expansion question. We are trying to get a broader picture... "Tell me more about that" "How would that work?" "What would that mean to you?"

When you are unsure about a given area or are unclear about what the client has said, you'll use a clarification question... "I'm not quite sure I understand..." "Can you give me an example?" "What exactly do you mean by...?"

When you want to change directions, you acknowledge the current issue and then ask a question that brings up a new issue. You are redirecting the conversation to an area not previously discussed. "Okay, I think I understand what you need here; could you tell me how you feel about..."

So when you begin questioning you'll ask your client to tell you a little bit about his business or his personal situation. When he responds, you're going to ask him one of the three types of questions. You'll ask him to expand on what he's said, clarify it if you didn't understand it, or you'll redirect him to a new area with one of the other exploring questions on your list.

Summarizing and Prioritizing

Once you've used the funnel technique and the direction questions to move through the explore phase of the sales process, you summarize and prioritize the customer's needs. Your customer probably has more than one problem or need. If you try to solve all the problems with one gigantic solution, you run the risk of scaring him off and losing everything. The best tack is to prioritize the problems and address them one at a time. This makes sure that you are addressing the issues that are of the most concern to your customer first. You'll also need to clarify his priorities within each area to be sure that the options you provide fit his success criteria.

The mindmap note taking technique we discussed earlier comes in handy here. You can use an asterisk, a checkmark, or even a different color pen to highlight each of the needs that have been identified. If you are selling phone systems, you might say, "Well, according to our map, you're expecting a sharp growth rate over the next 5 years so you definitely need a system that's expandable; your customers really depend on your being available, so reliability is a key issue; and most of your employees are not technical, so the system needs to be very easy to use." The key words you've highlighted on your mindmap are: expandable, reliability and easy to use.

If your client has a large number of requirements just keep highlighting them until the list is complete. Then ask your client to help you rank them. If it's a complex list of criteria and the decision will be made by more than one person, you might want to prepare a matrix including each person's rankings. This would give you a visual indication of the overall importance of each requirement.

End the Exploring step by summarizing and prioritizing the customer's needs you've uncovered. When you have finished conveying your observations, ask if she agrees with your evaluation. If you have been communicating well, there should be no discrepancy. You may want to state this as, "Do you agree with my observations of the problems you would like to solve?" On a more positive note, you might say, "Would you agree that these are the opportunities you are seeking?"

Also, clarify the customer's priorities within each area to be sure you understand the success criteria against which your options will be judged. Remember, the success criteria are defined as those factors by which the customer will judge whether your product or service is successfully meeting the customer's needs.

When you have several different decision-makers and influencers, it's not uncommon to find that each may have different—and sometimes contradictory—views of the situation. Prepare a chart including each person's rankings. This provides a visual indication of the overall importance of each success criterion.

There are times when you uncover many problems. If you try to solve all the problems with one gigantic solution, you run the risk of scaring him off and losing everything. The best tack is to prioritize the problems and address them one at a time. Delineate those problems you can help him with, which seem relatively unimportant and which ones you cannot help him with. Keep in mind it is always your option to seek other sources to help with those problems you can't solve directly. Once you have their rankings, you're ready to begin collaborating on possible solutions. The next section will give you ideas for making your collaboration sessions more effective.

STEP IV

COLLABORATING

▼

After you've worked with your client to identify needs and concerns, the next step is to determine whether or not your product or service will solve a problem or expand an opportunity for your client. Usually there are several different ways you can put your product or service together to meet the needs of your client. In the old, traditional method of selling, you would decide what was best for the client and then try to get him to see things your way. The competitive advantage way is much less adversarial and actually easier. You actually let the client decide which one of your options makes most sense for him... and then he buys it.

The first step is to collaboratively select the options that look like the best fit. Your client will have as much or more input into the creation and the selection of options as you do. This process ensures that he will be as committed to implementing the solution as you are. After all, why would he invest his time in creating a solution he doesn't want to buy? After you have jointly identified all the possible options, you can begin to weigh the advantages of each in a joint selection process. Once your client has told you which option best meets his needs, all you have to do is handle the details of completing the sale. What could be easier?

Life being what it is, the sales process generally has a few more twists and turns than that. But, if you are acting as your client's guide and you are guiding him down a path he wants to be on toward a goal he wants to reach, you will both reach the goal at the same time. And feel good about getting there! That's the beauty of the collaborative sales process—everybody wins. The client gets a solution that solves a problem or opens up a new opportunity and you make a sale and build a long-term relationship.

The next chapters will help you understand how to guide your client through the process of creating options and selecting a final solution.

CHAPTER 10

CREATING OPTIONS

▼

If you've done a good job of exploring the needs of your prospective customers, you've gathered more information than you could possibly analyze while you're sitting in front of the client. It's time to head back to your office to begin processing the information you've gathered, formulate some possible solutions, and prepare for your next meeting with the client. Before you leave the client's office though, set an appointment for a telephone call prior to your next meeting and an appointment for your next meeting where the two of you will select the options that will best meet your customer's needs.

At some point in your career, you've probably been told that if you're a good salesperson, you'll close the sale on the first call. Now, here you are, getting ready to leave and you haven't proposed a solution or asked for the order even once! The selling world today is very different from earlier days when your goal was to get the facts, propose solutions on the spot, and attempt to close all in one call.

Today, we face far more complexity in terms of customer needs, the products and services we offer, and the markets we sell in. This usually requires multiple calls.

But with some products, even in collaborative selling, a single contact may still be appropriate. Many companies today have provided their salespeople with sophisticated laptop computers and software so that they are able to explore a customer's needs, and create and select options all in one call—quite effectively.

This is the case with one of our clients, a major life insurance company. It has equipped its sales agents with highly advanced computerized technology, and this enables them to successfully explore needs and propose highly customized solutions—all in one call! If a company and its sales force have these high-tech selling tools, we're all in favor of a one-call sale. However, in this day and age, it's unfortunately the exception, not the rule.

It's up to you and your customers to determine the appropriate amount of time and the optimum number of calls for your selling situation. Although the focus of this session will be on multi-call sales, the ideas are just as applicable, with minor modification and creativity, in single call sales.

One indicator that it may be time for you to switch from a single call sale to a multiple call sale is when you find that you are making a lot of sales presentations but losing those sales to competitors. You may not be as thorough in your single presentation as they are with multiple calls. And remember, a multiple call design allows more opportunity for you to build the relationship over time.

Propose Multiple Solutions to Your Customer's Problems

When you get back to your office, you'll want to review your sales call and begin analyzing the information you've gathered. Your goal is to create several possible options that will meet your customer's need or solve their problem. Most salespeople make the mistake of proposing only one solution. This is a grave error for two reasons. The first is that you lose the client's involvement in creating the solution. If your clients are involved in creating the solution with you, they'll be far more committed to its implementation than if you create it without them.

You'll also find that your solution is far more likely to be on target if the client is involved in the entire process than if you do part of the process without their involvement. You may be an expert in your field, but they are experts on their business or personal situation. Creating a solution without their involvement at every step is a prescription for disaster.

The second reason for proposing more than one solution is that it allows the clients to easily see the trade-off of selecting different options. By presenting the pros and cons of each option, the client will be able to see that their ideal solution may not be possible. That's frequently the case in residential real estate transactions, cars and major purchases where the desirable options are often accompanied by a not-so-desirable price. Giving the client several well-defined options allows them to understand your rationale in making the recommendations you did. It also gives them the flexibility of mixing and matching possible options to come up with the best possible solution available.

Review your recommendations in light of what you learned about each topic area you explored, such as timing, budget, decision making criteria, politics, and so on. Ideally you are looking for a solution that will meet all of their success criteria. Usually, what you'll find, however, is that meeting one of their success criteria means that you may have difficulty meeting another one. For example in real estate, you may find a great home for your customer that meets their household living requirements, but you may not meet their criteria for quality of school system or proximity to shopping, or you may be able to meet all of the success criteria including school system and proximity to shopping, but doing so would put them over budget. By collaborating, the client will be able to help you solve the problem by telling you what is most critical and which factors can be subordinated to others. In other words, if your customer hasn't prioritized his needs already, he'll have to do it now. He may even need to re-prioritize in light of the possible options available to meet those needs.

The second thing to keep in mind when creating a solution is that wherever possible you want to create options that highlight those products or features where you have a competitive uniqueness or a competitive advantage. By designing your options and recommendations around your competitive strengths, you'll ensure that the competition will have a tough time bidding against you. They won't be able to meet the success criteria as well as you can, since you and your customer designed the criteria together.

Your third consideration when creating options is your company's constraints such as credit policy, deposit required, underwriting requirements, staff burden, delivery schedule, etc. It's much better to let the customer know these limitations exist up front than to get the order and have to go back later and explain why you can't deliver what you've promised. In a recent study by Forum Corporation, they found that reliability was much more valued by the client than responsiveness. That is, it's better to promise a little and deliver what you promise than to promise them a lot and then not be able to deliver it.

Collaborating on Flexible Products and Fixed Products

Flexible products and fixed products require different methods of creating solutions. A good example of a flexible product might be a computer. You can create a computer that is almost completely custom created, from components that are off-the-shelf. You can add memory, a fax modem, a bigger or smaller screen, different types of keyboards, a mouse and thousands of kinds of software to solve almost any problem. And if the software you want isn't available you can write your own, so finding the solution to your computer problem is relatively easy to solve. But let's say you sell only one line of laptop computers. There may only be one type of mouse or keyboard configuration available, or battery life may be limited by the size of the unit. These are fixed or semi-fixed products, meaning you can't change them just because an individual customer wants you to. Selling fixed products can get especially tricky when a competitor offers the feature your customer is asking for.

When selling a fixed product, you'll want to focus on those areas where you have advantages or uniqueness, and if your product excels in areas that are high priorities for the customer, be sure to highlight those. You may also be able to explore further to find out if those features where you have a competitive disadvantage are really something she needs or would use a lot.

And don't shortchange your value-added service package. Services like speed of delivery, maintenance, quality assurance books, reputation, training, extended warranties, and financing options can quickly turn a fixed product into a flexible product and make your solution the best solution.

Describe Your Solution Options in a Report of Findings

When you've figured out which options you'll offer to the client, you're ready to write your report of findings. We never write proposals. No matter what you say to the customer, they always look at your proposal as the only solution you could come up with. They view your solution as fixed and non-negotiable. No matter how much exploring you do, you're still sure to miss some details. Discussing the report of findings gives you an opportunity to discover anything you might have missed. Salespeople write proposals. Consultants write reports.

We recommend writing a Report of Findings that includes a section called Possible Courses of Action. In your report, you'll outline your understanding of their situation and you'll list their success criteria, ranked in order of importance. Then you'll list some possible solutions, including the options they have to choose from, and the pros and cons of each. Lastly, you'll create a one page executive summary. When it's complete, you'll be eager to share it with the client... but don't mail it!

Remember the phone call we scheduled in our last visit? Always call your client before your next meeting to review what you've come up with and to briefly discuss your rationale for what you're recommending. That way, if you are off target or something has changed since your last meeting you'll have time to adjust your report before your next in-person meeting. This is also a good time to get their input as to where they are willing to make trade-offs if necessary.

Never surprise your client with recommendations. Making the mistake of surprising clients—especially in front of their bosses or a committee—can be fatal. Even small surprises like a change in the price can make them look bad. Be sure to cover all critical areas on the phone. You might be asking yourself, "Doesn't that make the meeting unnecessary? If they already know what you're report says, why bother to meet?" You're not going to go over the entire report, just the highlights and the areas that might cause a problem to see if you can get some direction from the client as to the best way to proceed. The reason for the in-person meeting is to go over your report in depth and to discuss each option fully. Remember this isn't you proposing a solution but you and the client creating and selecting one together. Keep them involved every step of the way. That's true collaboration.

It's also important to confirm your appointment to go over the report in person. Don't offer to send them a copy before the meeting. If they request one, simply say that there are a number of things that you'll need to go over with them in person so you think it would be best to just wait for the meeting. And be sure to let them know that while there will be no surprises at the meeting, that there are a number of issues the two of you will need to discuss. Once you have presented a number of possible options to your prospect, it is very important to help him select the option that makes the most sense for his situation. The next chapter will give you ideas about how to guide the selection process.

CHAPTER 11

SELECTING OPTIONS

▼

After discussing your Report of Findings with your client and making any necessary adjustments, you're ready for your meeting to help your client select the solution that most clearly meets his needs. You may be wondering if your client won't be expecting you to present him with a final solution after all the information he shared with you during the exploring phase. Your customer is certainly going to expect you to be prepared... to be able to intelligently discuss the solutions you are presenting, but remember the customer ultimately wants control over the final selection. He'll want to leave your meeting with a solid rationale for his decision and remember, he may also have a need to explain his choice to his attorney, his boss or his team. Your goal in this meeting is to educate the customer and to collaborate with him to find the best possible solution for his situation and make sure he understands it well enough to explain it.

You'll want to check the degree to which each option addresses his needs and priorities, get feedback on each option and check the solution against the success criteria you discovered earlier. And remember, you've been telling your client since the beginning that you want to partner with him. Imposing a solution doesn't fit the partnering model.

Having the customer work with you to pick the right solution virtually eliminates objections and significantly reduces the need for price negotiation. Perhaps most importantly it makes commitment more likely and more natural for the customer, because he has ownership in the solution.

Reviewing the Options You've Created for Your Customer

When you meet with the client in person, start by reviewing the one page executive summary from your report of findings. It starts with a statement of the desired outcome and a brief review of the decision-making criteria and success criteria. Then there's a quick overview of the key options and your recommendation. This provides them with a "big picture" view of their situation. The overview is followed by the list of options to choose from in selecting the final solution. You will want to review the choices together.

It is often a valuable process to review key assumptions here, such as budgetary limitations or that fixed deadline that are not negotiable. Sometimes those assumptions limit the options you suggest and it's important for the client to understand the assumptions you were working under. Sometimes clients decide to remove those assumptions in order to expand their options.

You'll want to go from the most important decisions or options to the least important, or go through the decisions in chronological order depending on what makes the most sense in your situation.

Explain to your customer that you need his input on the likely outcomes that would occur if each option were selected. Then walk through each decision point using a technique we call menuing.

Menuing

Show the customer the menu of options and review the key pros and cons of each option. Ask your customer which option he feels would work best in his situation. Remember, there should be no real surprises here because you've already gone over the key decisions on the phone. You should be able to move quickly through most of the menus, but you may find it necessary to stop at one or two for some lengthy discussion.

One of the benefits of this method is that it allows you to discuss the price trade-offs of each of the various options as you go through the report. This helps you in three ways. First, the client gets to see the building blocks of the total price, so he has an understanding of where the price came from. Second, he is, in effect, accepting the price for the options he selects as you go along. Clients are generally less likely to balk at the final price if they created it step-by-step. And third, if they ask you to lower your price at the end you can revisit the choices they made and ask them which ones they want to change to lower the price.

This let's them know that you're not just going to drop the price, you're going to change the solution options as well if they are not willing to pay the price for the optimum solution. Using this method you'll get full price for whatever choices they select.

Many buyers who were trained in the old school will ask a salesperson today if they can negotiate the price. What they are really asking is if you can lower your price. In a true negotiation, you want to trade concessions, not just give them away. This method allows them to see that they can have a completely customized solution, but that they will have to trade-off something to get it.

Make Sure You are Collaborating with Your Clients

As you present your options, keep the client completely involved. If either one of you is dominating the conversation, you aren't collaborating. Some key questions you should be asking the client throughout the meeting are: "What other options do you see that I may not have considered?"... "What red flags do you see if we were to try to implement this solution?" and... "How do you see this option working in your environment?"

In traditional selling you would be getting objections at this point because you would be telling the client what he needed and he would be objecting to your solutions based on his knowledge of his situation. You would be acting as adversaries. In collaborative selling, you and your customer are partners looking for a solution that fits for both of you. You don't get objections; you get a review of needs and objectives. The customer may raise concerns about the appropriateness of any given option for his situation, and that's fine. That's what the collaboration process is all about.

You need to welcome this feedback as guidance in finding the best solution even if it challenges your view of the situation. It's critical that you try to learn from the client. They do know their company and its people better than you ever will and they are the ones paying for the solution. It's your role to help them find one solution that they can be committed to. Remember, it won't be the best possible solution, unless they're committed to it.

You want to encourage them to shoot holes in your solution and create some options of their own. Ask questions that will encourage them to challenge you. When you find that they have a concern in a given area, say "Let's explore the likelihood of that happening."... or ask "What impact do you see this having on your organization?"

Help them to relate their concern to the bigger picture and to their desired outcome. You might ask "Given your ultimate goal of X, how important is Z?" After a full exploration of the issue, including creating some new options, ask them which option seems most workable to them and then move on to the next menu item. At the end of the process selecting options with the client, ask what else would keep this solution from working. Is there anything else that would stand in the way of its successful implementation? Then, discuss with the client what else has to happen to get commitment and implementation.

If you truly can't find a workable solution for them, you may gain a COMPETITIVE ADVANTAGE by walking away. Admitting that you can't find a solution won't hurt your image, it will enhance it. All of the research shows that a customer would rather have you tell them up front that you can't help them, than for you to try, and fail. You promised them no pressure and no obligation, and you need to deliver on that promise if you can't solve their problem. You'll gain THE COMPETITIVE ADVANTAGE of trust and respect, and that's the toughest sale of all to make. Remember that your goal is to make a long-term customer, not a one shot sale. If together you cannot find a workable solution, walk away for now but keep in touch on an ongoing basis. Needs and goals change over time and you'll want to be there when the changes occur. With this type of sales and follow-up strategy, you'll eventually get the sale and create a customer for life.

A few years ago, a hot salesman in the computer industry sold forty million dollars worth of software in one year. The next year he sold four hundred million dollars and retired with forty million dollars in commissions at age 37. A significant portion of his business in the second year came as referrals from people whom he had told the previous year that he could not solve their problem with his software. Trust, respect and integrity do pay off in a customer for life who will happily and readily give you repeat orders, referrals and a reference whenever you need one. And it doesn't take many lifetime customers to build a happy and prosperous sales career. After you and your client have identified the solution that best meets his needs, finalizing the sale is generally just a matter of completing the paperwork. Sometimes however, a client will want a formal proposal. The next chapter will help guide you through that process.

CHAPTER 12

PROPOSING SOLUTIONS

▼

We believe strongly in the concept of partnering with your customer by creating and mutually selecting options. But from time to time, you may run across a customer who doesn't want to participate in the collaborative process with you and who just wants you to deliver a standard sales presentation. Of course, the first thing you'll try to do is to show him the benefits of the collaborative process from his point of view. But if that approach doesn't work, and if this customer chooses not to collaborate with you, you'll need to revert to a more standard method of proposing solutions. But, to a collaborative salesperson, even in this situation, the presentation is not a pitch; it is still a give-and-take exchange. It is a process of taking his ideas and combining them with your ideas to arrive at a solution that makes sense to both of you. The sales presentation in collaborative selling is not the slick, razzle-dazzle approach that some traditional salespeople use. Instead, it is a well-researched, customized presentation of realistic solutions to the prospect's needs.

Promoting the Unique Features and Benefits of What You are Selling

The best approach for proposing solutions is to take all the customer's needs and address them one by one, presenting the solutions as you go along. You can spend as much or as little time as appropriate in each area of the presentation depending on the client's needs. Your presentation should cover every issue that could possibly come up. This does not mean you need to discuss every feature with every prospect. On the contrary, you'll only cover those that are relevant. Point out the features and benefits that make your product or service superior by focusing on your competitive strengths.

Your presentation should be clear and well organized. The order in which you present the features and benefits will depend on what you are selling and the priorities of your prospect. With some products, there is a natural or logical order in which to show or discuss the features. In addition, there may be an advantageous place to end. For example, when a Realtor shows a house, she knows there is a natural order that most people follow when they tour a home. If you are selling a product that does not dictate a natural order of presentation, use your prospect's priorities as a guide.

Keep in mind the primacy and latency effects. Primacy is presenting your big guns first so they'll be remembered. Latency is presenting them last. The best combination is to start big; give your most salient features and benefits first. When you give the benefit summary, however, leave one of your best features for last.

Let's talk a little about how you'll handle features and benefits. First, let's define them. A feature is some aspect of the whole product that exists regardless of a customer's needs. A benefit is the way that feature satisfies a customer's specific need. *A benefit is a feature in action.* Most customers think in terms of benefits. They don't care how it works, they want to know what it will do for them; how will it solve the problems they are having.

Of course, you can always present a feature and its corresponding benefit, and then repeat the process for each feature and benefit, but that tends to bore your customer and it makes you sound like every other salesperson. We prefer to get the prospect involved by using the "Feature/Feedback/Benefit" method. Using this approach enables you to get feedback from the customer on the appropriateness of each major feature and benefit your solution can deliver. When discussing the features of a house for example, you might say, "This house has a kidney-shaped swimming pool and a Jacuzzi." How important is that to you and your family? You give the feature and ask for feedback. This allows your customer to actually create his own benefits for the feature. You'll often find that they will come up with benefits you would never have come up with on your own.

A realtor was showing a young couple a house. When she pointed out that it had a fireplace, the young woman smiled and said that she had always wanted to have a fireplace she could use as a planter! There is no way the realtor would have come up with that benefit on her own.

If the customer doesn't come up with the benefits you have in mind, you can always point them out. But the benefits they come up with themselves are usually the ones that are most important to them. If they do come up with all the benefits you have in mind, you don't have to say anything. You can just move on to the next feature.

When customers come up with their own benefits, they are confirming the importance of that feature in their own mind and they are establishing its value. Which pattern you follow to review features and benefits will vary, however, depending on the level of knowledge of the customer and how technical the options are that you're discussing.

Here's an example following the basic pattern of feature/feedback/benefit for a knowledgeable customer, but in this case, you'll start with a statement of their specific problem. You'll then present the feature, and ask for feedback. Because the customer is knowledgeable, you'll encourage her to provide the benefit.

You might say, "I know you've been running out of storage space on your existing computer." (Statement of the problem.) "This model has a 200-megabyte hard drive." (Feature.) "Given your current and future requirements, how do you think that capacity will work for you?" (Request for feedback.)

The customer responds, "That will give me the storage space I need and then some for quite a while. It sure would be a relief not to have to worry about that anymore." (Benefits.)

Sometimes, you have customers whose needs and priorities are clear, but their technical knowledge is limited. In this type of situation, it may be better to go with the benefit first, followed by the feature, and then request feedback. Here's an example for a customer who has said downtime is costly:

"This mainframe has been able to reduce downtime caused by system malfunctions by up to fifty percent over comparable models." (Benefit.)

"This is because it runs its own self-diagnostics routine every twenty-four hours."

(Feature.) "Would that downtime savings be significant for your operation?"

Your customer doesn't need to be a technical wizard to give feedback on the importance of eliminating downtime, yet this process still keeps him involved.

Whenever possible, encourage the client to come up with his own benefits. If he comes up with important benefits that match your features, he'll be selling himself. Keep these feedback questions in mind to involve prospects in your discussion of the solutions to his problems:

"How do you see this fitting into your situation?"

"What other advantages do you see in this?"

"This is how it fits into your business; how do you see it fitting into your family life?"

"How do you see this addressing the opportunity we discussed earlier?"

"How well does this look like it will meet your needs?"

Remember that any feature can have more than one benefit. And, any desired benefit can be achieved by more than one feature. When pointing out each, be sure to cover all the relevant possibilities. It's not unusual to have the prospect interrupted by an employee or a phone call during your presentation. When the prospect hangs up the phone or the employee has left, avoid the temptation to reiterate what you have covered so far. This gives the impression that you are summing up for the end of the presentation. Instead, briefly review the last point you made and then continue the presentation.

If there are too many interruptions, you can point out the situation to your prospect. He might be able to change it. Place the blame on the environment by saying, "It seems pretty hectic around here today. Is there someplace we can go to grab a cup of coffee and finish this?" That may be all he needs to either take you up on your offer or have his secretary hold all calls and interruptions for the next half-hour or so. You can then enjoy his undivided attention. If that doesn't work, a last alternative, and perhaps the least desirable, is to offer to reschedule the appointment.

How to Structure a Presentation to a Group of Decision Makers

Here are a few helpful hints you can use when you have to meet with more than one decision-maker in a group presentation. Your presentation, depending on the size of the group, may be less flexible than a one-on-one meeting. The larger the group, the more structured your presentation will become. It may not work if everyone jumps in with their feedback and ideas simultaneously, so a semblance of order has to be arranged. You'll want to structure the presentation and provide for a question and answer period in the middle of the presentation.

If you ask for questions at the end and there are none, the silence can be awkward. If they ask a particularly tough question and that you can't answer or if you answer it poorly, you may leave them with a weak impression. By putting the question and answer period in the middle of the session, you can come back strong and finish on a high note. The end of your presentation should be like an attorney's closing argument. You'll want to focus their attention on all of the positive highlights of what you've just presented and end with a benefit summary and high energy.

The ideal situation is to have most or all of the decision-makers involved during the exploring phase. That way they will have contributed to the success criteria and the points you discuss will hit on thoughts they have expressed regarding the problems and opportunities at hand. There will be times when you will have to give a presentation to a group of people who were not involved in the previous phases of the sale, but who need to hear your proposal in order to give their blessings to the sale. This type of group presentation will be more formal than the one-on-one.

You should tell them your name and company and explain in one clear, concise sentence the premise of your proposal. For example, your statement might sound like this: "Good morning, I'm Jeff Baxter from International Hospitality Consultants. I'm here to share with you my findings based on my research of your company and my discussions with Mary Farley that suggest my company can help you increase your convention bookings by 15 to 30 percent."

Give a brief history of your company and its qualifications and credentials. Mention a few companies that you have worked with in the past, especially if they are big names. This serves to "ground" the client and let's them know who you are and the extent of your experience and credibility. Have copies of an account list available for everyone in attendance. Hand out copies either in advance or while you are talking. This list will show them the various sizes, locations and types of companies you've helped in the past. Succinctly tell the group where your company stands vis-a-vis the competition. Don't get into a detailed analysis of comparative strengths and weaknesses; just make it clear how you compare to your competition by focusing on your competitive uniqueness and advantages. If your company has an impressive money-back guarantee or an extended warranty, mention it.

After you have established the credibility of your company, begin getting the group involved in the presentation. Get everyone's input into the success criteria and decision-making criteria. Preface this with, "I've spoken to Fred, Sally and Sue and gotten their views on the changes they would like to see in this area, but I'd like to get some input from each of you on this matter." Get each person to add to the list of optimal benefit and decision-making criteria. Take notes, perhaps on a flip chart, on what they say because it will shape your presentation.

After everyone has had a chance to speak, go through your presentation exactly as you would in a one-on-one presentation. The primary difference is you want to be sure to answer all the questions, fears and concerns that come up in the group. Meet each of their specific needs, whenever possible.

When you use this method, it is essential, during your preparation, to brainstorm all the possible concerns and questions the decision-makers may come up with. This information will come from talking to people within the company, fellow sales people and other people in the industry. You should be so prepared that there is little they could come up with that you haven't already thought of and prepared for. If they do come up with something, you might say, "Let me research that and I'll get back to you." Then make sure you do it!

When you prepare for a group presentation, prepare a notebook with data, specifications, reports and solutions to specific problems. It should address everything you and your prospect discussed in the exploring phase: problems, success criteria, decision-making criteria, etc. and how your product or service answers each. At the end of it, include support documents and copies of testimonial letters. Do not read from the notebook. It is strictly a resource of facts to give your prospect after a decision has been made. Do not expect to cover every point, unless it can be relatively brief. Remember: Documents don't sell products, people sell products. Your notebook will in no way serve as a substitute for a first-rate presentation.

The notebook should not contain prices. There are several reasons for this. First, some people will go directly to the prices without reading through your solution. Second, prices tend to prejudice non decision-makers who should not be concerned with prices. The third reason is politics. Imagine a group of decision-makers who have not had a raise in two years looking at a document that proposes a two million-dollar expansion plan for the company. You're there to solve problems not create them.

Make it clear that you are not trying to hide the prices and that you would be more than happy to talk about them with anyone they wish and that you simply wanted to respect their privacy on what can sometimes be a sensitive issue. As a backup, you'll want to have copies of the investment summary on hand for each of them if they request them.

Ideally, you should find out before the presentation if they are responsible for dealing with the financial aspects of the purchase. If so, you will have to talk about the costs and the benefits they'll receive in relation to the costs. When you give your presentation, address each problem and give specific information about your solution for each one. Make sure you discuss features and benefits and get feedback from the group. Ask things like, "Can you see any other advantages to this?" or "How do you feel about that; do think that would solve the problem?"

At the end, provide a benefit summary. "Here is what you will get if you accept my proposal..." Talk about how the benefits will address their specific needs. At the end of your summary, ask if there are any questions. When someone asks a question that is answered in your proposal document, refer her to the appropriate section of the document and assure her that a complete answer is provided. Solicit the impressions of the group. Ask if they agree that the solution you proposed would solve their problem or meet their needs. The point is: Don't be afraid to ask questions.

Using Audio/Video Demonstrations to Enhance Your Presentation

Let's discuss the art of demonstrating. A demonstration, like a photograph, is worth at least a thousand words. Videotapes, slides, audio sound tracks and live demonstrations are fun, effective and keep the pace of the presentation moving. A demonstration aids in learning. By making your points vivid, you make them .memorable. Associating new information with images that are already familiar will cement the bond and guarantee the impression. Analogies, especially humorous ones, are potent aids to memory.

It is important to make the demonstration relevant. Don't assume the prospect will be able to visualize and appreciate the use of your product or service in her business unless you show her. This is especially true of technical, industrial and office products.

When setting up a demonstration, be certain all the key decision-makers will be present. Produce something of value for them to take home. Give everyone, but especially the user of the product, a chance at hands-on experience. Point out the benefits of its operation. And finally, provide an oral or written summary of the information you want them to retain.

Preparing a Bid with Your Proposal

When you are asked for a sealed bid along with your competitors, it's even more important to learn everything possible about that prospect than if you were going to collaborate with them. There are several things you can do to give your bid more impact. First, if you can, sell your prospect on letting you write the specifications of the product or service. Non-technical buyers often look to vendors to help them with the specifications. You should be able to write them in such a way that they will favor your uniquenesses and advantages. Second, present an extensive comparison of your offerings vs. your competitors. Be sure you are comparing apples with apples so that your comparison is valid. Third, meet the specifications and then add something extra—your competitive advantage. Describe what your company can do above and beyond the competition. All of you may have a similar product or service, so you have to offer extra benefits such as an extended warranty, specialized customer service, or a different financial package. These offerings can significantly alter the total cost of ownership. Fourth, include a list of references so your claims can be corroborated. The key to submitting and winning a sealed bid is to differentiate your product. It must have more perceived value while being priced the same as or less than your competitors. And finally, include testimonial letters with your bid. These demonstrate the extra value of your product or service.

A salesman we know sold football equipment to high schools. His sales included big contracts based on sealed bids. He always included at least three testimonial letters from schools who absolutely loved him. They loved him because he or a member of his staff would always go to their football games and sit on the sidelines with a box full of helmet pads. He did this because everyone knew the pads became compressed when the helmets were hit a few times. When the kids came off the field, he would change the pads for them. He considered it part of his contract to supply the helmets. Coaches liked buying from him because they didn't have to deal with injuries and lawsuits, and he also eliminated the need for them to maintain the helmets and to keep parts on hand. The extra value he added and the letters attesting to it worked wonders for him.

Summing Up

Traditional sales people often worry about the presentation because they see it as the only time to really "sell" the prospect. Collaborative sales people don't worry. They know that if they have done their homework and maintained the relationship along the way, collaboration is simply another step in the sales process. The collaboration process is made infinitely easier because they've invested the appropriate amount of time to explore the prospect's situation and are confident that they can propose attractive solutions.

Let's briefly review the steps in Collaborating. Remember that we said earlier, if you want to be successful in today's market, you must be able to get the buyer's attention. To do that you must be able to differentiate yourself, your company and your product. The Collaborating phase is where you do that—where you really differentiate yourself from the rest of your competition...

Collaborating begins with the attitude that you and your customer are going to work together to create a solution to a problem, or to create more opportunities for their business. After you've explored the prospect's needs and concerns, you'll create a Report of Findings that contains multiple options or possible courses of action.

Your report becomes the basis of discussion for your next meeting with the customer or for a formal presentation to a number of people involved in the decision-making process. One of the advantages of having a "menu" of options is that it allows you to discuss price tradeoffs as you go through the options.

Throughout this process, you'll be asking open-ended questions. "How do you see this option working in your environment?" or "What do you see that I haven't considered?" When you're making a presentation to more than one person, you'll need to address the concerns of everyone present. When they ask a question, ideally, you'll be able to refer them to a section of your report that addresses it.

It's very important for you to distinguish between the features and the benefits of your product or service. A feature is built-in... it's there whether the client appreciates it or not. A benefit is only a benefit to the client. When you make this distinction, and learn which benefits a client hopes to achieve, then you won't waste time pointing out features in which they have little interest.

When you demonstrate your product, be sure all the key decision-makers are present, and that they will each have something of value to take home. (For instance, if you're selling commercial ovens, give each prospect a loaf of bread baked in it, to take home. That way you'll be involving all of their senses in the decision.) If possible, give the customer a hands-on experience and provide a summary at the end of all the information gained during the demonstration.

And finally, if through collaboration, you cannot create a solution that works for your client, acknowledge it. You may gain a competitive advantage by telling the truth and walking away. In today's marketplace, the advantage of integrity cannot be overestimated.

In the next section, we discuss the next phase of The Competitive Advantage—the one many salespeople consider the most difficult part of the sales process—confirming the sale.

STEP V

CONFIRMING

▼

In this section we're going to discuss some very important points about gaining true commitment from your client... how to make a lifetime customer, not just a sale. If you've done your job properly in the first four stages of selling—Target, Contact, Explore and Collaborate—your customer should ask to buy from you! If you've been conscientious throughout the sales process, collaborating closely with your prospect, you should naturally progress to the commitment process together. The commitment becomes a how and a when, not an if. So we call this phase confirming, not closing, the sale.

A study by Forum Corporation showed that the sales superstars seldom use a close at the end of the sale, because they are confirming throughout the collaborative sales process. In fact, in 46% of their sales, they never had to ask for a commitment. It's analogous to asking someone to marry you. If you're unsure of the answer, don't ask; it's probably premature. When collaborative salespeople do ask, it's usually no more than a nudge. Because they are always in step with their customer, the transition from selecting solutions to confirming is natural. Signing the order is just a formality.

Before you confirm the sale, you'll want to be sure your prospect has all the information he needs to increase his perceived value of your product or service. Make sure he understands exactly what he will be getting before, during and after the sale. Review all the key benefits you'll be providing and relate each to his success criteria. This summary at the end of the collaboration stage will make the transition to confirming easy. Then simply ask for the commitment using an open question that seeks direction, such as "Where do we go from here?" or "What's our next step?" or "How should we proceed." This type of question leaves the control of the sales process where it belongs... with the prospect. No pressure is created. These are straightforward questions that keep your prospect participating in the collaboration process. This method allows your customer to feel that she "bought" rather than being "sold."

CHAPTER 13

DEALING WITH ACCEPTANCE
AND REJECTION

▼

Throughout the sales process, you should always be listening to the questions prospects ask you. They are clues to what the prospect is thinking. The questions salespeople love to hear are the ones that signal intent to buy including: What credit terms do you offer? Can I try it one more time? How much lead-time do you need? How does the installation process work? How soon could training be started?

When you hear these musical questions, your response will lead into a natural process of taking care of the sales logistics... order forms, contracts, checks, and so on. If you've developed a good solution and you've established that it's within their price range, the buying commitment should be a natural outcome.

However, sometimes the positive buying questions don't come and your client starts to back away from the process. There's something wrong... either the prospect isn't giving you complete information or you've missed something along the way. What do you do?... back to the questions! Candidly ask what's blocking the decision. The collaborative sales process isn't designed to put pressure on your customers. It's designed to solve their problems or help them to take advantage of opportunities. It's what you've done up until now that will make or break the sale. If your customer isn't sold by now, more pressure won't do it. What's needed is more specific communication about what they need, or what you have to offer. That's why we ask open-ended questions like "Where do we go from here?" or "How should we proceed?" and "What do you see as our next step?" You're asking the customer to tell you what else he needs in order to move the process forward so you can implement the solution you've created together.

The sales process we're showing you is a very natural process of two, or more, people sharing their information to develop a solution to a problem or need. It requires trust, respect and open communication on both sides. You can't work as partners through all the stages of the sale and then at the end, try to use a manipulative closing technique to clinch the deal. It doesn't make sense.

One of the reasons a traditional close sometimes works is that the constant pressure on the client forces him to tell you what's really holding up the sale. But if you can get the same information by communicating openly and honestly, there is no need for the pressure. Getting acceptance for a sale means you've done a good job of collaborating. You can go on to assuring—the final segment of the sale. What happens when you don't get an unqualified YES at this point?

It's possible that you may have to prod your customer to tell you what's really blocking implementation of the solution you've worked out together. Don't be afraid to ask for open honest communication about what's happening. The client promised honesty and full participation in the beginning, remember?

In traditional selling, the salesperson asks "closed" questions meant to force the prospect to say "yes," such as the forced-choice or the sharp angle close. The salesperson tries to take complete control of the situation and the customer at precisely the time when the customer most wants her autonomy. She wants the right to make her own decision without being railroaded into a decision by the salesperson... even if it was the decision she was already going to make. Pressure creates problems in the sales relationship. To reduce the pressure, the prospect may create a smoke screen.

A smoke screen is something that obscures the relationship or the decision-making process. Common ones are "Your price is too high," and "I want to think about it." Both may indicate that your customer is uncomfortable communicating their uncertainty—they're avoiding telling you their true feelings and thoughts. Your customer may also engage in the "objection game" where they try to think up more objections than you can possibly overcome. This is a "no win" game and a signal that there is a problem with the relationship. A thousand closing techniques won't help you here. They'll only irritate your customer and destroy the trust and respect you've built. And listen to the way it sounds when you say you are going to "close" your customer. How would you like to be "closed?" It sounds like it's the end. Instead you should simply change focus. Using our marriage analogy, the previous stages represent the courtship... confirming is the marriage ceremony. That's the point we're at now. Assuring, which we'll discuss in upcoming chapters, is what we'll do to make sure we'll stay together long-term.

When you get a yes, you should always review the solution and its benefits... develop a complete implementation schedule... and clarify the customer's expectations and success criteria. This covers things like terms and financing options, payment schedules, delivery schedules, training dates, warranty periods, servicing procedures or anything else that might not have been covered when the prospect was selecting options. The prospect has now become a customer. You want to welcome him into the family and help him learn how to use his new product or service to his best advantage, and how to get help if something goes wrong. You want him to know that you will be there for him.

By the time a salesperson gets to this stage using the process we've discussed, there is a high probability that the proposed solution will be accepted. However, there are also some reasons why it might be rejected. We live in a rapidly changing environment—priorities change, people move, people lose their jobs or suffer a sudden loss in the stock market. Companies merge, go out of business and change directions... sometimes overnight. The person who had the authority to purchase your product yesterday may be in a different division tomorrow. What all this change means is that in some cases, by the time you get to the end of the sales process, you may find that there is no longer a need. In others cases, you may find that you have to start the whole process over again from the beginning. But most of the time, if you've done a good job of exploring, creating and selecting options, you'll find that things go just as planned and you'll be settling the details and beginning a new customer relationship.

In those rare cases when you do lose the sale, you'll want to make sure you don't lose the relationship. If things fall apart at the last minute, you can express your disappointment at not getting to work with the client, and support him as much as you can in whatever decision he makes. Even if he's buying a competitor's solution, offer to give him whatever help you can. The competitor's solution may not work and the customer may come back to you later for help. Let them know that you will be staying in touch.

Use the final minutes of the call to pave the way for the next call, if there is to be one. Note any commitments you made such as price quotes, delivery dates or terms discussed. Above all, be sure to let the client know that you want to maintain the relationship. Ask him for a post-sale analysis of specifically what you could have done better. You will impress him with your seriousness about being able to offer better service.

If you consistently ask for a post-sale analysis, you can begin to catalog the answers and spot trends or problems that you can avoid in future sales. Make notes following each call so you can evaluate your performance. Doing that after confirmed sales will point out your strengths. For lost sales, you will discover your weaknesses by evaluating what transpired, how it affected the outcome, and how it differed from your success pattern. When you get back to your office be sure to enter the follow-up date in your tickler file, write a thank you note, and put this customer on your mailing list.

At the end of your day, sit in a quiet place, reflect on the call and use a visualization process to improve your performance. Run the "tape" through in your mind and envision what you did. Then imagine the scene again, but this time see yourself doing everything perfectly. Imagine the prospect's reaction to your new behavior. And remember, it's essential to finish by visualizing a successful outcome. Let go of your mistakes. Trial and error is how all human progress is made. Focus on and hold a picture of yourself successfully completing each sale.

Visualize your successes often. By doing so, you will reinforce the successful and effective things you do. Your mental repetition of productive behaviors will create strong working habits.

Even if you have performed the sales process perfectly, at some point you are going to experience barriers to the sale in the form of customer concerns. We used to call the objections and we tried to knock them down, run them over, or trick the prospect into forgetting about them. Now we know that those concerns are a vital part of the process and how we handle them determines the strength of our long-term relationship with our customer. The next two chapters will give you important techniques and information for handling customer concerns.

CHAPTER 14

ADDRESSING CUSTOMER CONCERNS

▼

We've talked about what to do if you get a "yes" or a "no" from a customer. But sometimes you get a "maybe." What do you do if you've asked an open-ended commitment question that seeks direction from the client and he tells you he wants to think about it before he gives you a commitment? You check the five customer concern P's: Price, Priority, Politics, Personality, and Postponement. Let's look at each one in detail. First... Price.

Clarify the Customer's Price Concerns

Price always seems to be a major hassle. Theoretically, it should seldom come up because you should have covered budgets, payments schedules, financing options, etc., during the exploring and collaborating stages, but financial situations and competitive situations can change dramatically overnight. When price does come up, be sure to clarify what your client means by price. Let's say you're a Realtor selling a house for $100,000, and your client tells you that your price is too high. He could be saying that he thinks the house is worth $100,000 but he can only afford to pay $75,000. In this case, you might respond by redirecting the discussion to monthly payments rather than the total purchase price, try to do some creative financing that would make the house more affordable, or find him a house that's more in his comfort range.

However, when a client says the price is too high, it may have nothing to do with affordability. Instead he may mean that he doesn't really think the house is worth $100,000. In this case he's concerned about the value he's getting for his $100,000. We could respond by letting him know of all the special features and upgrades in this house that make it worth the price. He might also mean that compared to other houses he's looked at he doesn't feel this house is worth $100,000. Here it's important to be sure he's comparing apples with apples, such as quality of neighborhood, school systems, quality of construction and so on.

The client could also mean there's someplace else he'd rather spend his $100,000... that this particular house is not worth $100,000 to him. That gets us into priorities that we'll discuss in a minute. He could be saying that he thinks the house is worth $100,000 to someone else, but not to him because it's too far away from his job... or he doesn't like the view... or whatever. If this is the case, you'll simply add that new information to his selection criteria and find him a house that better fits his needs.

It's also essential to differentiate between price and total cost. Price is what you initially pay for a product or service. It's a one-time charge. Total cost is what you pay over the term of the ownership, the recurring expenses. Total cost takes into consideration resale value, maintenance costs, performance guarantees and operating costs. Considerations such as after-sale appreciation, depreciation, or operating costs can significantly alter total cost. For example, with a car phone you pay a price for the equipment and the airtime. The total cost, however, includes the quality of the network and the equipment, customer service and responsiveness, sales support, and other services to enhance the usage of the car phone such as a voice mailbox, call forwarding and hands free usage.

Other price concerns include the size of the down payment, how payments match cash flow, interest rates on financing, forms of payment accepted, tax deductibility, and other financial considerations. Sometimes, rather than trying to guess all of the possibilities, it makes sense to just say, "I sense you have a concern about money. In an ideal world, how could we structure the financial package to best meet your needs?" Then work from there to see how close you can come to meeting his financial requirements. Usually, you only need to get reasonably close to get the sale. This is a good way to help the client get at what's bothering him about the financing.

So, obviously it's important to know what a customer means when he says, "Your price is too high." It's critical to clarify their concern before you respond.

Understand Your Customer's Priority

The second "P" is Priorities. This one also covers a lot of ground and in my opinion is really the most important of the "P's". We've all known of a family that had little to eat or wear, yet they always had a new car or a new color television set. The same is true in business. If there's one thing we've learned about selling, is that if your product or service is high enough on the priority list, nothing will stand in the way of the sale. The mistake many salespeople make is focusing too narrowly when they define their competition. It's not just others in your business; it's anything else they might buy that would make the money for your product or service unavailable. It's important to establish your product at the top of their list!

This is where knowing the customer's style, values and selection criteria come in. Does the customer tend to move toward or away from particular outcomes? Is their primary need for prestige or practicality? How will they be comparing this purchase to others possible investments. Will it be return on investment, cash flow generated, payback period, cost savings, revenue generated, budget availability, political considerations or even personal convenience? Clients may not even be aware that they are using a particular criterion, so you may have to ask a few questions to determine what it is, but they always have some way of sorting alternatives.

Don't underestimate the power of priority. If you can get your product or service at the top of the list you can almost guarantee a sale. All of the other "P's" pale by comparison to the power of priority.

Recognize Problems with Decision-Making Politics

Let's talk about the next P: politics. Most salespeople believe they should just stay out of it and sometimes that's exactly the right thing to do, but typically there are two scenarios you'll have to deal with. The first situation is when your product or you are the political issue; the second is when your client or his project are bogged down in politics. If it's your client or his project that's stuck, you'll act only as an advisor. You're primary goal will to be to help him come up with some options for gaining internal support. The more options you create for him, the greater the possibilities he'll have for getting it unstuck. Perhaps you can help him to find out what criteria others are using to put their project ahead of his. Then it's just an issue of priorities.

The best way to deal with you or your product being a political football is to head it off in the beginning of the sales process. You should be building support for you and your project right from the start. By finding out who all the players will be and making them active partners in the process, you should have already identified and worked out the politics by the time you get to this point in the sale. If you haven't, you'll need to start at the beginning with these other players, just as if nothing at all had been done. Be completely open and honest with them and dig for their concerns and reservations about the project. Work hard to take their concerns into consideration when you're creating options and selecting solutions. Bring them through the process until everyone agrees to move forward.

A frequent problem with this approach is that your client may not let you speak to the others involved. He may prefer to handle it himself. If this happens to you, ask your client what decision he would make right now if it were solely up to him. If he tells you he would pass on the project, you still have some selling to do with him. You'll need to find out which aspects of the solution aren't working for him and create some new options. If he tells you that he would buy if it were up to him, then ask him how you can best help him to sell his project to others.

Politics don't just apply to business sales scenarios. They can also arise in a household where a husband and wife or a parent and child are vying for control. One situation we observed was where the husband was ready to write a check for a new "family" car while ignoring the input and concerns of his wife and kids. His wife told him that if he bought the car without taking into account his family's input, he could drive it alone. The salesperson was caught in the middle of this political power struggle and couldn't make the sale until it was amicably resolved, fortunately with his subtle and sensitive relationship skills.

Avoid Personality Conflicts with Your Customers

So far we've covered Price, Priorities and Politics. The fourth "P" is Personality conflicts. This may be the most important concern to handle immediately and well. Your relationship with your customer is the foundation upon which everything else is built. If the relationship collapses, so does everything it supports. This happens because somehow trust was broken—your sales style may not have been appropriate for the prospect's buying style or the prospect may not feel that you have a sincere interest in his needs. The way your client learns to trust you is when you do everything you say you'll do when you say you'll do it. Each time you don't fulfill a promise, your client trusts you a little less. Each time you do what you promised, your client trusts you a little more.

Another common personality conflict is no confidence. The best way to deal with the problem of no confidence is to never let it happen in the first place. If you're sincerely trying to help your clients, no confidence rarely happens. Listen more than you talk, always monitor how well you're doing with your clients, and always... always... always do what you say you're going to do when you say you're going to do it. When there are problems or glitches, make it right. Stay on top of their ever-changing needs so you can alter your offerings appropriately.

Whatever the cause for the personality concern, you need to use all of your communication skills to get the relationship back on track. You should assess the prospect's style and make every effort to treat him in a way that matches. You might want to review the four styles— Dominant Directors, Cautious Thinkers, Steady Relaters and Interacting Socializers that were presented in Chapter 6.

You may even need to ask if there is a personality problem during a meeting. The way to ask such a direct question is to say, "My philosophy is that if two people want to do business together, the details never stand in the way. Let me ask you this; given where we are and what we've been through, do you feel comfortable enough with me to want to do business?" If the answer is yes, you can review your prospect's needs to make sure you're both in agreement.

If the answer is "no" you'll have to ask the client if he believes it's possible to get your relationship back on track. If he says "yes" you'll need to pay careful attention to what he's requesting, and be sure to fulfill all of his requests. If he says no, thank him for his candor and request permission to turn the account over to another salesperson. The best way to do it is to tell the prospect that you want to get someone involved who can better meet his needs.

When you think about the sales process, try picturing yourself and your prospect in a maze together. You're both trying to get to the prize in the center. But you can only see the left side of maze and your client can only see the right side. If you lose touch with your customer, neither one of you will get to the center. If you stay together and communicate, you can both see everything and together you'll get to the center easily.

You're going to try a lot of options before you find the right one and you'll have to stay with your customer, even if he makes a turn that you think is wrong. Eventually he will realize that he's gone down a blind alley and will start back. To meet your goals both of you need information the other has. If the customer has a concern—it's because he can see something you can't. So you need to find out what he sees so you can start to make progress again. Only through communication and teamwork can you both win.

The last "P" is postponement and it's one of the most challenging objections to deal with. The next chapter will give you several ideas for moving from postponement to a sale.

CHAPTER 15

DEALING WITH POSTPONEMENT

▼

You have been working with a prospect through the sales steps and are confident that you have a solution that meets the client's needs so you ask an open-ended commitment question and get a maybe instead of the definite yes you expect. Stay calm and just review the five "P's" Price, Priority, Politics and Personality Conflicts and Postponement. We discussed the first four in the previous chapter. Now it is time to handle postponement... it's perhaps the trickiest of them all.

We don't like to call the five P's "objections" or even resistance because as a collaborative salesperson, you'll only encounter resistance if you're in an adversarial environment. If you find yourself in an adversarial environment, the first thing you'll need to do is try to change the environment. To change the environment, just be open with your client about your perception of the environment. Remind your client that you want to be his partner and that you are only interested in selling him something if he really feels it will benefit him and his organization.

When you're in a collaborative environment and the relationship is working, you won't get objections or even resistance. But you may get some form of postponement. It's very important to find out the exact reason for the postponement. The client will probably say something like, "I appreciate all your work and it looks like a good solution but I'll need some time to think it over."

That doesn't tell you much. There could be many motives behind a statement like that and you'll need to find out the real reason for postponing the commitment.

Understanding Your Customer's Personality Style

Under postponement you've got four more P's... Personality Style, Product, Personal comfort, and Policy. When we say personality style, we're referring to Relaters, Thinkers, Socializers, and Directors, and this is one area where really understanding the personal style of your customer is important. Cautious Thinkers and Steady Relaters are both Indirect, which means they proceed slowly and cautiously. They avoid risk and they want to make sure they make the right decision.

Relaters typically need to check with their team before they'll feel comfortable making a decision, so you'll need to encourage the Relater to involve others throughout the sales process, not just at the end. The Thinker may want to thoroughly review the details of your proposal or might need additional data before he can make a decision.

The Cautious Thinker is an interesting style to study because most buyers, at times, act like Thinkers. If it's a major purchase or if a wrong decision could jeopardize their career, many buyers adopt a cautious, analytical approach to a buying decision. So it's important to know the steps to take with any cautious buyer. Remember that their dominant pattern will be to move away from the things they fear. You'll want to show them that they can solve their problems by moving away from the things they don't want.

First, you have to make sure the customer has all the information he needs. If he doesn't, ask what additional information he needs to make a sound decision and offer to gather the information for him. Try to stay involved in the information gathering and evaluation process. The closer you stay to the process, the more you will be in touch with any changes of direction or additional needs that might be uncovered. Ask the customer to inform you of any change in needs or focus. Remind him that you are partners in this process.

Ask the customer to identify the date by which his examination of the solution will be completed. Ask if there is a deadline for the decision. Don't push—but do ask. If there is a decision deadline, it gives you a reason to stay in touch and offer additional help or information. Staying in touch during the decision period is critical. If he says his deadline is May 23rd, ask if you can call him on May 24th if you haven't heard from him first.

Offer to help the customer with anything he needs in order to get support for his solution. Sometimes this means helping with a presentation to the board, setting up a demonstration, arranging a trial period or providing a money back guarantee. Remember, with Thinkers it's essential to lower their perception of risk. Sometimes customers just want to do a sanity check. A sanity check is where the customer thinks your solution is the right decision but they want to bounce the proposal off 2 or 3 other people to make sure they haven't overlooked any key decision points. It's their last chance to ask, "Am I missing anything?"

With the other styles, a delay probably indicates a problem and you'll need to uncover the reasons for the delay. "I need time to think about it," may seem like a door closing on the sales process but your ability to ask questions can keep it open.

Good questions for uncovering reasons for a delay are, "Which parts of the report are you unclear on?" or "Which options are confusing you?" or "It was my understanding that you were working against a deadline—is that still the case?" or "What specifically can I do that would help you with this process?" or "Will you be looking at the merits of our solution compared with another or will you be comparing the priority of this project with other projects in other areas?" or "Do you already have a source for the cash or will you be looking for one?"

Direct questions like these will keep the door open and the sales process moving along. Let's face it, no matter how much exploring you do; you still may have missed something. Don't just leave your partner there to figure it out by himself. Ask the tough questions that will get the process unstuck.

Overcoming a Customer's Concern with Your Product

The second postponement "P" is product. If your customer has concerns about your solution, you'll need to explore them. Sometimes he'll tell you straight out that he doesn't think your product will meet his expectations or success criteria. When this happens, you know that something went wrong in the exploration or collaboration stages. Somehow, a high priority need was not identified during exploring or you forgot to show how it would be met by your solution when you were selecting options. You'll need to go back to the Exploring stage to discover what was missed and then proceed again to the collaboration stage.

When the resistance is due to a technical problem beyond your control, use the compensation method. Acknowledge the deficiency, but try to compensate for it by pointing out other features and benefits that outweigh the shortcoming. For example, if you cannot meet a delivery date, suggest other times and stress the advantages of another date. This method is effective when the shortcoming is not of paramount importance.

Another option is the boomerang method. Think of what a boomerang does. It is thrown out, makes a wide arc and returns to the person who threw it. You can do the same thing when you react to resistance. Imagine a prospect saying, "We are too busy right now to put your product into service." The boomerang response might be, "The fact that you're so busy makes time-saving all the more important to you. We have already agreed that my product will save you 50 percent of the time you are currently spending. If you invest a little time now to install it, you will find yourself with more time at the end of the month than you expected."

As an alternative try changing the premise. In this case, you take the premise on which the prospect is basing her response and change it so she can see it in a different light. For example, the prospect says: "This won't accomplish the XYZ process." Your response could be, "When we first spoke you said you liked our product because of its convenience. We then discussed the fact that it might also accomplish the XYZ process as a secondary benefit. Is convenience still your number one priority? If not how would you rate the relative importance of each priority now?"

Assess Your Customer's Level of Personal Comfort

The third postponement "P" is personal comfort. These are often the toughest to diagnose. Your client may tell you that they aren't really sure what the problem is... that they just want to think about it. Usually they are concerned about the risk involved. Try to find out how they perceive the risk of your solution. One good technique is to have them list the pros and cons from their point of view. There are several ways you can reduce their perception of risk. If you offer a money back guarantee, now is the time to reinforce that message and talk about the specifics of how it works. Perhaps your solution is based on a new technology that management has been resisting. You might be able to take the customer to see a successful implementation in another company or talk to one of your other customers on the phone.

You might offer a pilot project to let your customer sample the product or service in a limited way before proceeding with the entire project. A pilot is where your customer commits to the entire project but roles it out only one stage at a time. A stage might be one location, one new computer, one plant, whatever. After reviewing the results, they would role out the whole project as is, make changes or cancel the balance of the contract. A small pilot project allows you to prove to your customer that everything you have said about your product and service is true.

How you handle payment in a pilot can be critical. If they don't have to commit and pay up front they will be more likely to look for holes in the solution because if it works they will have to write a big check. They will also be more likely to view it as your solution and not their solution. Ask the client to commit to the project and place the entire order with the stipulation that if the pilot doesn't go well he can cancel and get a full refund for the unused potion of his order. Once they have made the financial commitment, your client and others in his company will work hard to ensure that what they've already committed to works out.

If your client insists on shopping around before he'll commit, make him a better shopper! Assuming that you've done your job and that you have a good solution, you'll want to make sure that he is at least as demanding of other potential vendors as he has been of you. Help him identify the key factors he should take into account and help him develop a list of questions to ask. Explain the significance of each question to his situation.

Provide information on your competitors, including strengths and weaknesses. This is an excellent opportunity to highlight your competitive advantages and uniqueness. Volunteer to serve as a consultant or a sounding board, answering any questions that come up as the customer shops. Help the customer compare and evaluate the other solutions gathered. Ask for his commitment to discuss the findings with you when he's through shopping but before he's made a final decision.

The fourth postponement "P" is policy. You'll handle it almost the same way as you handle the customer who wants to shop around. Occasionally, you'll run into a customer who really wants to buy your solution but his company has a policy that requires getting three bids for everything purchased. Help write the specs if you can, and then do everything else just as you did for the shopper.

Getting a Psychological Commitment from Your Customer

Sometimes you'll find that even though your customer likes your solution, he'll just want to make sure there isn't something better out there. Maybe you're the first salesperson he's talked to. If this is the case, it's often effective to offer a tentative confirmation. The customer commits to buy your product but reserves the right to cancel under certain specified conditions. Many travel agents use this method to travel arrangements. Even though you're not bound, you've made a psychological commitment to take the trip. That psychological commitment stops the shopping process and your customer will have a higher comfort level knowing that they can cancel if they decide to.

An example of psychological commitment happened when a neighbor wanted to get a pool built in his backyard. The pool salesperson gave him a really good proposal. He liked it a lot but he didn't feel comfortable signing the contract without checking around. The salesperson told his client that it would take 15 days to get the necessary permits and offered to go ahead with the permits if the client would sign the agreement. This allowed our neighbor, the client, time to shop around for those 15 days and cancel if he found something better. He signed the agreement and never did get around to doing the comparison-shopping!

Many salespeople are very flexible about what they allow the prospect to write into the contract. Clients may say they want to check with certain people and that any one of them can have veto power, or that if they can get a lower bid they can cancel without penalty within a certain period of time. Experienced salespeople don't worry about it because they know the prospects are just getting comfortable with their investment decision and covering their downside risk. Usually within a few days, they've forgotten all about their concerns and are working hard to make sure that the solution they created is implemented in the best possible way.

How to Find Out the Reason for Postponement

There may be times when you are unclear about exactly what's causing the postponement. If you find yourself in this situation you can always use this simple four-step process: Listen, Clarify, Resolve and Confirm. Listen: hear the customer out. Listen carefully for clues as to what the real concern is. Remember that you need to completely hear the concern before you can respond.

Clarify: question to make sure you have a complete understanding of the concern from the customer's point of view. What do they mean when they say they aren't sure your product or service will meet their needs or they're not sure it will work in their environment?

Then move to Resolve: respond appropriately to the concern. Your response will obviously vary depending on whether their concern is product, price, priority or politics.

Finally Confirm: Make sure that your solution did resolve his concern. The worst mistake you can make is to move on thinking you've solved a problem that still exists.

Listen... Clarify... Resolve... Confirm to get unstuck.

Another great method for resolving customer concerns is to develop a script. This is a set of detailed responses to common customer concerns that each salesperson develops for her product and company. One way to develop a powerful script is to have all the salespeople meet and come up with their most frequently encountered customer concerns. These concerns are discussed one-at-a-time with each salesperson describing his or her most effective response. The responses that seem most useful to each salesperson can be added to their personal scripts.

When you discover many concerns expressed repeatedly, find ways to pre-empt them during the presentation. Top salespeople build the answers or responses to these common concerns into the sales process before the client ever brings them up. This eliminates the concern before it becomes a real concern to the prospect. But all concerns can't be covered in advance or the sales presentation would go on forever and would bore the faster-paced prospects. So you need to have strong, well-thought out responses to all possible customer concerns.

A blunt statement is difficult to respond to. You can, however, convert the statement to a question and answer it. For example, to the statement, "I don't think I could use that product," you could respond, "What I hear you wondering is, what benefits would this product bring you?" You can then proceed to answer the question, not rebut the statement.

Summing Up

Integrity in business is essential and it dictates, among other things, that you work towards win-win solutions with everyone. Managing resistance is simply using different forms of logic to help you be a better consultant. There will be times when your prospect does not see her problems or the solution to her problems clearly. It is your job to gently and diplomatically return with her to a point of agreement and begin again from there.

Dealing with a customer's postponement is a major part of the sales process. Although postponement is a challenge, it's a workable one. Once you have successful worked through the postponement concern and the customer has confirmed the sale, you face your biggest challenge: making sure the customer receives excellent service from your company and from you. We'll deal with techniques for meeting this challenge in the next section on assuring the customer.

STEP VI

ASSURING

▼

Step six in the collaborative selling process is Assuring. Even though this step happens after the sale is closed, assuring is the real secret to long-term, extraordinary success in sales. Many salespeople today believe that their job ends when they get the sale. They disappear from the customer's life, leaving service, installation, training and follow-up to someone else. Unfortunately, they also leave their repeat and referral business to someone else.

Making sure your customer is happy with his purchase is the dividing line between good salespeople and the stars. Master salespeople know their success depends on a customer who is delighted the day he buys the product, happy with the purchase decision a week later, completely satisfied with the product and service a year later and committed to you and your company when it's time to repurchase whether that's two years later or ten years later. A customer is a lifetime asset. The hardest part of the sales relationship is building the initial trust level. Master salespeople keep their relationships strong through outstanding service and support. Their efforts pay dividends through repeat purchases and referrals.

The next chapters will guide you through the process of assuring the satisfaction of your customers. It will give you important tips for servicing your customers, enhancing the customer relationships and expanding your business opportunities.

CHAPTER 16

SERVICING THE CUSTOMER

▼

When we are working with our clients' salespeople, and we ask them to develop their statement of competitive advantage they often become frustrated, just as you may have at the beginning of this book. They tell us that they can't claim that their product will cut costs by 20% or increase productivity by 10% because they've never measured it! If you don't measure the success of your products, services and solutions, who will? When you do measure, make sure you measure what's really important to your customers. It may not just be quantitative measures. Peace of mind, lower stress levels, closer family ties, and increased enjoyment are all good qualitative measures to monitor. Be sure to measure time periods that are appropriate for your product. For example, insurance agents, stockbrokers, and financial planners wouldn't want to measure dividend performance or investment results on a short-term basis.

You'll find that measuring results will provide some significant advantages for you. Perhaps most important, it solidifies your relationship with your customers. If results are good, they'll be glad to tell everyone inside and outside their company about you. If the results are bad, don't despair. Remember, you and your clients are in this together. You created the solution together, so you'll need to work together to solve any problems that arise. Either way, it's good for the relationship.

Measuring also automatically sets up your next sale. If your results are good, you're in a great position to recommend buying more, upgrading for even better results or buying another product not yet discussed.

Third, you'll be quantifying your successes. Imagine a year from now being able to say with confidence that your product can cut costs by up to 40%! That's a real attention getter and it's even more compelling when you can present the data to back up your claim.

If you're serious about being a sales professional, you'll need to start documenting your successes today. If you're going to claim to be better, you have to be ready to prove it.

Following Up After the Sale

There is an adage in traditional selling that says "the sale begins when the customer says no." We believe that the real work of selling starts when the customer says "yes." If you'll take the time to determine the lifetime value of just one of your customers, it will help you to understand just how valuable this step is. Stew Leonard, CEO of the world's largest dairy store, believes that every customer that walks through his doors is worth $50,000. Automobile companies have valued one loyal customer at $140 to $350 *thousand* dollars! A 20 year client for a fee-based financial planner can easily be worth over $100,000.

In business-to-business selling, one lifetime customer can mean many millions of dollars in revenue! You have a huge responsibility if you're handling that kind of an account. Take a few minutes today to calculate the lifetime value of your accounts. You'll quickly see what it costs to lose just one customer.

At the beginning of the sales process, you have the potential to build a good customer relationship, but it's after the sale that you really have an opportunity to solidify the relationship.

You make sales by making promises to your prospects. You make customers by delivering on your promises. You make lifetime customers by delivering on those promises consistently.

So... what does it really take to make sure your customer is happy? First, be absolutely clear on the criteria your customer will use to judge the success of her purchase. You should be thoroughly familiar with her success criteria by the time the sale is made. If not, this is the time to establish them. Simply ask the customer how she would know a year from now whether this had been a good decision or a bad decision. Ask for specific, measurable criteria. Then, monitor and measure the degree to which those criteria are being met.

You have to stay in touch. One approach we like to use is the 1-5-15-30 follow up schedule. We call it that because you'll take specific follow up action 1-5-15 and 30 days after the sale. Of course, this schedule is a guide. Product implementation cycles vary, so your schedule should be adjusted accordingly.

Day 1: Your follow-up starts with a thank-you note immediately after the sale. A short, handwritten note is all that's needed... something simple and sincere like, "Dear Mr. Jones, I really enjoyed helping you choose your new telephone system. I trust that it will give you years of service and I look forward to working closely with you to ensure that it does."

Day 5: The next follow-up, approximately 5 days after expected delivery of the product, is just to make sure the product has been received and that it's working. This check-up call is especially important to identify any initial problems. If your computer customer hasn't been able to get his favorite software to work on your computer, he may be blaming you, your computer, or your company for a problem that could be fixed in five minutes.

You may find that your customer isn't using your product yet or that they are not using it fully. This should raise an immediate red flag for you. There may be a training or installation problem or it may be nothing, but be aware. Products that aren't being used could kill your future business. When you get this response, be sure to schedule further follow-up.

Day 15: Approximately 15 days after the customer receives the product, call her again. This follow-up lets the customer know you're still available and that you still care about her satisfaction. Above all, it tells your customer that you value her relationship even after you've made the sale. By this time, she has received your thank you note and this is the second call she's received. She should feel well taken care of. If she is still happy with the product, she should be delighted to give you referrals.

Day 30: Approximately 30 days after the sale, send a gift... a little something extra. It doesn't have to cost a lot but it should have a high-perceived value and be related to the purchase. For instance, a health club might give new members sweatbands imprinted with the club logo; a computer company might give its customers some public domain software or a diskette storage box. A real estate agent might give new owners a plant or a nice picture of their new home to share with family and friends.

The gift need not be expensive and ideally it should be a conversation starter. One of our clients sells car phones and customers a pen shaped like the car's antenna. Customers love these unique mementos and they keep them on their desks. When others see them, they pick them up and ask about them. This invariably leads to a conversation about cellular phones which frequently leads to another referral for the salesperson.

Operations-Driven vs. Customer-Driven Salesperson

Successful sales people are customer-driven rather than operations-driven. It is essential to understand the difference in the two orientations. Salespeople either focus on serving primarily the customer, thus being *customer*-driven, or focus primarily on serving the company, thus being *operations*-driven.

The operations-driven salesperson tends to be *product and business* focused, always looking for ways to sell the product and make things easier for himself and others within his company. He encourages systems and procedures to protect himself and his company. The customer-driven salesperson, on the other hand, is *customer* focused, always looking for ways to make things easier for his customers. He helps create policies and procedures that are "customer-friendly."

The operations-driven mentality is "How can I *sell* something?" and thus uses a product/feature focus. The customer-driven mentality, on the other hand, is "How can I *help* people?" using instead a customer/benefit focus.

Operations-driven salespeople have their eyes solely on the bottom line trying to maximize profits on each and every transaction, while the customer-driven salesperson keep his eyes on the customer and understands the long term value of a customer, thereby maximizing long-term revenues and profits.

In an economic downturn, the customer-driven salesperson survives by creating a competitive advantage and uniqueness that makes people want to do business with him. He knows that people will be willing to pay more for goods or services if they are getting more value. In contrast, the operations-driven salesperson is left to focus only on price.

Understanding these basic differences between an operations-driven and a customer-driven salesperson is essential if you are going to make a positive change toward being more customer-focused.

The First Step: Commitment

What should the *function* of a customer-driven salesperson be? The obvious answer is "To make money!" While that answer may be obvious, it isn't the correct one. Making money is the *goal* of salesperson, not his function. The *function* of a customer-driven salesperson should be, as

Ted Levitt of the Harvard Business School says, "to acquire and maintain customers." And "to acquire and maintain customers" successfully requires the first key to strong customer relations—*COMMITMENT.*

COMMITMENT to customer-driven service must permeate all of your actions and, ideally, all of the actions of your company. Are your actions and the actions of your company focused on doing *whatever it takes* to make your customers happy? Are you committed to the complete satisfaction of your customers? Are new employees in your company quickly and thoroughly oriented to the customer-driven philosophy? Does every employee understand your company's customer-driven philosophy and *know how to implement it on a day-to-day basis?*

Can every employee in your company explain what their job *really* is? Often employees believe their job is strictly typing or delivering or collecting overdue bills; consequently, when they get a call from a customer with an unusual request or a problem, they view it as an interruption of their "job." If, however, every employee in your company knows that their primary function is to get and keep customers, and that every other task in their job description must take second priority, then your business is truly customer-driven.

A company that wants to be truly customer-driven must put everything—its time, money, efforts, words, meetings, slogans, training sessions, and behaviors—behind its commitment to getting and keeping customers. This means that every company employee must do what it takes to accomplish that primary function.

Such commitment isn't something that just you as a salesperson should feel strongly about, nor is it something that should be felt by only management and the key staff members. Everyone, no matter what their daily tasks involve, must be completely committed to superior customer service. When every member of a company is committed to superior customer service, *they know what makes exceptional customer service is, they know what it looks like to the customer, and they know what to do to provide it.*

Key Principles of Customer-Driven Service

Let's look at some of the key principles that help define customer-driven service.

People do not buy things, they buy expectations. You must get as much information as possible about the expectations of your customers. A lot of businesses lose because they believe that a customer buys "things." But, as an example, a customer doesn't simply buy a computer, a thing that is nothing more than an electronic box. A customer who is in the market to buy a computer is buying a *solution to certain problems*.

If you deal with customers simply on a level of "things," their evaluations and decisions to buy will be based primarily on price. If customers view the product as a commodity, whether or not it is, they are going to judge it primarily based on price. If, however, customers see your product or service as a *value-added* product, then they will be willing to pay more for it because it is not just a commodity.

Close contact with customers must be maintained. Because you know a lot about your business, you may frequently add products or services without fully understanding your customers' needs—what they want, what they need, and what expectations they have. Gather as much information as possible prior to designing solutions with your products and services.

By going out into the market place and having face to face conversations with your customers, you can stay close to them by learning the intimate details about what's really important to them, why they do business with you, what they like and don't like, and what they'll buy and won't buy.

Remember that customers' needs are dynamic, not static. Your customers may come to you for a particular reason, but as things change or their businesses move ahead, their needs change. If you respond only to their initial reason for coming to you, and not to their current needs, you may provide them with the wrong solution and lose them as a customer.

When two people want to do business together, they will not let the details stand in the way. People want to do business with people they like and trust. When you have a strong relationship with your customers and a problem occurs, their attitude is, "*We* have a problem. How are *we* going to handle it? But, when you and your customers do not have a strong relationship and a problem occurs, their response is, "*You* have a problem and what are *you* going to do about it?

Creating Moments of Magic… or Misery

Every interaction you have with a customer can be described as a *Moment of Truth*. When an interaction falls short of a customer's expectations, a level of customer dissatisfaction—a *Moment of Misery*—is created.

When an interaction exceeds a customer's expectations, that's a *Moment of Magic.* Your challenge is to make *Moments of Magic* out of as many of your interactions with your customers as possible. If you want to build a base of exceptionally satisfied customers who will go out and speak positively about you and your company, and who will literally urge other people to do business with you, you must create consistent *Moments of Magic.* When you do, you create demanding customers— those customers whom you have treated so well with your superior service, that they are now spoiled. You have raised their level of expectations.

Why create demanding customers? Doesn't that mean more headaches for you? Think about it for a moment. If your customers know that you will take care of them—spoil them—then they are a lot less likely to go looking elsewhere to do business. This creates severe headaches for your competition, not you, because the competition generally cannot keep up with the high service standards you have set and that your customers have become accustomed to receiving. Whenever one of your "demanding" customers comes in contact with your competitors, they pale by comparison to your company. There are many examples of companies that deliver consistent *Moments of Magic* for their customers. Nordstrom's, a retail store, is legendary.

Customer-driven companies attempt to create *Moments of Magic* with every interaction they have with every customer.
- They set up systems and procedures to ensure that their customers do not experience problems but in fact experience Moments of Magic with each and every encounter with their business.
- They develop quality products and services with strong guarantees.
- They hire dedicated employees, train them well, measure their performance, and reward them when they consistently provide superior customer service.
- They design customer friendly systems and technology.

In other words, customer-driven companies and customer-driven salespeople try to do things right the first time, every time.

But, even such customer-driven companies stumble once in a while and create a *Moment of Misery.* Complaints come up, problems happen. The *Moment of Truth* that turns that misery to magic is how that problem or complaint is handled. The best customer-driven salespeople and companies rise above the rest of the crowd by exerting extra effort to *quickly* solve the problem and assure the customer's satisfaction. Sometimes all it takes is something minor—sometimes it takes something major. But when you can turn a *Moment of Misery* into a *Moment of Magic,* you take a giant leap ahead in terms of customer satisfaction. Statistics on customer service show that when you *quickly* resolve a customer problem, you create more customer satisfaction than if nothing went wrong at all!

The customer-driven salesperson constantly measures customer satisfaction and stays in touch with his customers. Of course, you're opening yourself up to potential problems when you start creating "demanding customers" by talking about measurement, commitments and expectations. But in today's highly competitive environment, if you're going to survive, you have to have an excellent product and even better service. If you can't meet your customer's expectations, you aren't going to be in business very long.

If you discover that your customer's expectations haven't been met, first look at whether the solution you've chosen is completely unworkable or just needs an adjustment in your customer's implementation plan or perception. Usually, if a customer's expectations aren't being met, the reason falls into one of four categories; product failure, implementation error, buyers remorse, or selective perception.

With product failure, something has happened to the product—it isn't working physically or mechanically. The customer will be happy with it as soon as the defect is fixed. But it's critical that we make the correction quickly and cheerfully.

Implementation or User Error could be almost anything—sometimes the product is working but the customer doesn't know how to use it or how to use it properly. Thousands of software packages didn't make it because they were too complicated to use, because their manuals were hard to read, or because the right training wasn't available. It may be an over-used word, but user-friendliness is a key criterion for success with any product. Other implementation errors might include your customer not getting along with your trainer or installer, or maybe you've missed a deadline. Most often it is simply the inability of the client to properly utilize your product or service because of their lack of training. Many sales involve the installation of a new system or piece of equipment. Naturally, the buyer or his employees must be trained to use it. Given the fact that people tend to forget 75 percent of what they've heard after two days, it is not surprising that user error is a common cause of dissatisfaction after the sale.

Achieving your customer's success criteria will hinge on the effectiveness of the training. It's imperative, therefore, that you follow-through after the training period to make sure your customer is using the product properly. The more complex a product or service is, the better the training must be. Computers are a perfect example. It often takes new computer users weeks or months before they can use their systems quickly, smoothly and to full capacity.

If user error is a common problem in your business, you should consider training your prospect before you confirm the sale. There are two advantages to this:

1. You reduce user error to practically zero. A well-trained customer will achieve his success criteria immediately or very soon after the sale.
2. Your prospect will be psychologically predisposed to doing business with you based on the time and energy he has already invested in your product.

It is unlikely that someone would learn how to use your computer, for example, and then repeat that training to compare it to another. It's just too time-consuming. In addition, to learn the second system he must unlearn yours. That may make it seem like your system is easier to operate. Once your customer is comfortable with his new skills and your equipment, he's much more likely to buy your product.

User error is not limited to the world of high technology. There's an old story about a farmer who went into a hardware store to buy a new saw. He asked the owner for the best one in the house. The owner showed him a beauty and claimed it would cut five cords of wood a day. The farmer bought it, took it home, but returned a week later with it. "I'm sorry," he said to the owner, "but no matter what I do, I can't seem to get more than four cords a day out of this saw." The owner took it from him, "Well, let me see if there's anything wrong with it." He reached down, pulled the starter cord and the motor roared to life. The farmer jumped back and said, "Wait a minute, what's that noise?" You can never assume people know how to use your product. Take the time to demonstrate it and to train them.

Salespeople often underestimate the power of buyer's remorse. Buyer's remorse is the regret someone feels after making a purchase. Selective perception, user error or just an uneasy feeling that he will not realize the full benefits of the product or service can cause it. Buyer's remorse could also be caused by the economic strain caused by the purchase. Until they've had more experience with your product, your customer may question whether the benefits will prove to be worth the investment. When a customer either directly or indirectly expresses some regrets in having made the purchase, calm his fears by assuring him that his investment was wise. Repeat the success criteria and the time needed to achieve them. Remind him that employee training and other factors take time to impact performance. If all else fails and you sense your business relationship will suffer, talk to your company about allowing the customer to return the product, if that is an appropriate solution. If your customer is truly unhappy it's better to give up your commission and still have the good will.

Selective perception is the process in which a person sees only selected details of the whole picture. For example, your customer may have purchased a new copying machine that works like a charm, but she is irritated by the sound of the motor. She chooses to focus on what is wrong rather than on everything else that is right. Selective perception occurs because buyers expect their purchases to be perfect. Regardless of the purchase price, they figure they deserve perfection. And they do, within reason. When you run across someone who is experiencing selective perception, resolve the problem by pointing out the compensating features and benefits. Paint a brighter picture. Put the negative detail in a different perspective so it becomes an insignificant part of the total picture.

Selective perception can apply to many things: performance characteristics, product operation, product idiosyncrasies, minor inconveniences, down-time and the customer's idea about what the solution to a problem should be. This is well illustrated with one of our client's experiences. Bob Adamy is the owner of small hardware store near Buffalo, NY. Bob tells a revealing story about a customer who purchased a Toro tractor. "The customer called me up two years after he bought it. He was ranting and raving because his tractor broke down. I said to him, 'Tell me what you want me to do and I'll do it for you.' The customer demanded his money back. I tried to discuss some other options, but he wouldn't budge. So I wrote a check for the entire amount of the original purchase and told the customer that one of my assistants would deliver the check and pick up the tractor.

My assistant came back an hour later and asked me to step outside. In the parking lot was my flatbed truck with the customer's tractor on top. Sitting on the tractor was the customer, who had refused to budge.

He had the check in his hand. I said, 'I thought you told me you wanted your money back.' He said, 'No, what I really want is go get my tractor fixed. I love this tractor!' So I told him, 'Well, if you just get down, we'll take it off the truck and put it in the shop.' He said, 'No, I'm not getting off this truck. I just want my tractor fixed.' So I got a mechanic, got the parts, fixed the tractor right on the truck, took him home and got my check back."

Bob's approach to customer service has paid off well. He is now one of the top ten Toro dealers in the country, even though the floor space he has allocated to Toro is relatively small. Bob also has one of the most impressive records for market penetration; a full five to ten percent higher than Toro's penetration in other areas of the country. He is so highly valued by Toro that they asked him to be in their training film with Arnold Palmer.

Summing Up

The moral of the story is: if you go out of your way to provide good service to your customers, they won't make outrageous demands. All they really want is a good return on their investment. In return, they will pay you back repeatedly with referrals and additional purchases. These customers are truly annuities. If it's not just something simple, you'll have to collaborate with the customer to solve the problem. Find out if their situation has changed, if your assumptions were wrong or if the product was just a poor match for their needs.

The very worst possibility is that it was just a poor solution to the customer's problem. You can't hide, if you ever want to do business with this customer again. None of us likes to face problems, but studies show that when a customer problem is addressed and fixed promptly, the customer is actually more loyal than if the problem had never happened. They've tested your reliability and found a supplier they can count on.

Problems give you a chance to show how much you care about the customer. To handle them, you need to immediately acknowledge the problem and take responsibility for your part in the problem. Then you have to do whatever possible to resolve the problem. This could be anything from a letter of apology to a partial or total refund. Confirm with the customer that your solution was a satisfactory one for him. And whatever you're going to do... do it quickly. Speed is essential when a customer has a problem. Too many companies say no, no, no and then, after they have lost all customer goodwill, they say yes. Saying yes up front will go a long way toward building customer loyalty.

If your customer has a major problem, you may need to return to the exploring, collaborating and commitment stages to find the solution which will best meet your customer's needs. You may also have to make significant concessions in order to keep this customer.

Keep in mind that it generally costs 5 to 7 times as much to win a new customer than to retain an old one... and remember the value of just one lifetime customer. There is more at stake here than the profit on one sale—all future sales and all future referrals from this customer depend on your ability to reaffirm your commitment to quality and service. As a professional salesperson, your customers aren't just part of your career; your customers are your career. The next chapter will give you ideas for enhancing your customer relationship.

CHAPTER 17

ENHANCING THE CUSTOMER RELATIONSHIP

▼

Conducting an Annual Review with Your Customers

Let's now focus on the annual customer review. We've found that even salespeople who are good about sending thank you notes or a gift after the sale usually don't do an annual review. An annual review can be a major part of maintaining your relationship with your customers. A lot can happen in a year... people move, get married, have children, change jobs, develop new needs. You have to stay in touch. If the only time you talk to your customer is when you're asking for more money or another commitment, they won't feel that you have their interests at heart. The annual review is a good time to catch up with them and make sure your product is still meeting their needs. You'll often find that your client will ask for your help in areas not discussed previously.

Like any successful meeting, an annual review requires a little planning to be most effective. Arrange for the meeting to take place in an area that is quiet and conducive to conversation. Take notes and send a clean, typed copy to your client within 24 hours. Be organized—have an agenda of what you want to talk about. Bring all of the records you'll need to discuss the previous year's business. If there are areas where your company fell short of expectations, discuss those first. Outline what steps have been taken to correct the problem. If your company has a quality book, now is a good time to show them how you'll prevent such problems in the future.

Most importantly, listen carefully for the customer's stated or implied needs, concerns, and opportunities. This meeting provides a perfect forum for the customer to air grievances, share compliments, and discuss wins and losses. Your actions demonstrate that you are interested in maintaining an open, trusting partnership with your customer. Reinforce this at the end of the annual review by saying something like "Ms. Jones, I appreciate your insurance business, and

I want you to know that I will continue to work hard as your insurance consultant to meet or exceed all of your expectations."

At the end of the review, offer a new idea, service, product, or promotional deal when possible. This is an excellent opportunity to spark interest in something new or to thank them for previous business.

The annual review is a key way to enhance your relationship with your customer. As in any relationship, continued open communication is essential. However, you should anticipate problems whenever possible. You should always be alert to the warning signs of customer dissatisfaction such as a decrease in rapport, a sudden decrease in orders, or an increase in complaints. If you're suddenly hearing rumblings about price, quality or service, you'd better act immediately.

Sometimes you get a clue that the customer is less than completely satisfied with your product or service when he starts to talk about the merits of the competition. He might ask you if you've heard about the upgrade just announced by ABC Corp. Sometimes you'll notice a coolness coming from your customer—maybe he doesn't return your calls or he's too busy to go to lunch. Maybe he doesn't share information as openly as he did previously. His change in behavior may not have anything to do with you or your product, but you'll want to check to be sure. Changes in your customer's personal life, such as a divorce or separation, arrival of a new baby or death of a parent can also impact your relationship, especially in the short-run.

One event that cannot be overlooked is when there is a change in management or ownership. When a new manager arrives, she wants to make her mark as quickly as possible. She may have loyalties and relationships to other vendors that she wants to bring with her. This is her team. Be sensitive to her needs for comfort and control or you won't be on the new team. It's critical to begin building a new partnership with her. Remember, you are starting over so begin right at the beginning of the sales process just as if this were your first call on the company. Getting her "big picture" view and future orientation is essential.

Another thing to watch for is a big change in sales volume. That could signal a change in the market or in the industry. You need to be aware of developing trends—whether they are problems or opportunities —so you can respond to them. Large increases in orders may also signal financial problems. There is no need for alarm but you may want to alert your accounting department to be sure. Managed properly, this situation could actually work in your favor.

Monitoring Your Customer's Ongoing Needs by Keeping in Touch

In the exploring phase, we talked about the difference between the customer's desired situation and current situation. This is called the need gap. Our goal during exploring was to have the customer discover for herself how large her need gap was. The larger it was the greater her desire to take immediate action to "close" it, hopefully by starting to do business with you. It's important not to forget the need gap during the assuring phase of selling. Here, we want to make sure that the customer perceives that her need gap "closed." If so, she'll have little desire to talk to your competitors. But, if her need gap is getting larger instead of smaller, especially if it's due to your lack of customer attention during the assuring phase, she's much more likely to respond positively to your competitors' advances, and you stand a good chance of losing the account.

The little things mean a lot in maintaining contact with your customers—like sending them interesting articles, introducing them to people who might have similar interests professionally or socially, sending birthday cards or product anniversary cards, or just calling to see how things are going. Keep a customer profile of their interests, likes and dislikes and keep adding to it. Reviewing it periodically will give you many ideas for keeping in touch.

Why not stop by periodically just to check on how your products or services are functioning. Because you see your equipment in a lot of different environments, you may be able to offer tips and suggestions for improving efficiency. One of the best ways to stay in touch with what's happening with your customer is to talk to others in your company who have regular contact with the client—your technicians, trainers, customer service reps, etc. They can tell you a lot about how well the product is working for the customer because they work directly with the users inside your clients company. Schedule regular meetings with these people to review your customers' files. Use them as your early warning system to alert you to problems and opportunities.

You might want to start a newsletter to share new information or ideas from other clients who use the same products. You can also include articles or ads about new products or complimentary products. Many companies sponsor user's group meetings so their customer can share ideas with other customers.

One way to solidify the partnership is to include your clients in a focus group or quality control board. You might even put together a panel of clients who would help you to design your next generation of products. When your customer hires new employees, offer to set up a training session for them. Remember, those users will be influencers for the next round of purchases. What better way to make sure they're on your side than to train them from the beginning?

Encourage your clients to call you at any time with ideas, questions, grievances, jokes, and feedback... whatever's on their mind. Many top salespeople make it a habit to give customers their home phone numbers. You want to make sure that the lines of communication are always open, and that there is more than one link between your customer's company and yours. The more points of contact between the two, the stronger the bond. For example, if your customer's head of engineering knows your service technician and feels comfortable calling him directly, it strengthens the relationship between the companies. Think of each relationship as a single strand in a thick cable that connects the two companies. Even if one or two of the lines break, the bond will still be strong and will hold until the broken strands are repaired or replaced.

After the sale is made, there are two things to keep in mind: The first is: "Out of sight, out of mind." If your customers don't see you or hear from you frequently, they will forget about you. Conversely, by maintaining regular contact, you will be the first person they think of when they need something new. The second is: "What you don't know can kill future sales." If you don't know that your customer has taken a new direction or that his company has been acquired, you are probably going to lose this customer.

Enhancing the customer relationship is really just a matter of communicating regularly—listening to his needs, providing him with evidence of your interest, and making sure he has everything he needs to meet his success criteria for your product. Your role as partner is to do everything you can to make your customer successful... because their success is your success. The next chapter will help you understand how to leverage your sales through your conscientious application of the six steps of collaborative selling. The results of your efforts pay off in a truly competitive advantage.

CHAPTER 18

EXPANDING BUSINESS OPPORTUNITIES

▼

The customer service techniques in this chapter take some time and effort to implement, but they're not only worth it... they're the keys to success if you want a career in selling. The salesperson who collaborates with his client to find the right solution and then follows that up with excellent service, establishes a strong partnership with the customer. That close partnership puts you in the best position to take advantage of new sales opportunities when they arise, and it enables you to expand your customer base inside and outside your customer's organization.

Look for Opportunities to Sell More to Your Current Customers

If you are in your customer's home or company frequently, following up with service or training or just dropping by to talk with your customer, you will find clues to new opportunities. These opportunities could be additional products or services your customer needs or they could be opportunities in other parts of their life or their organization.

You should always be thinking "account penetration." Are there any other products or services that would make your customer more successful? Could your customer take advantage of discounts by ordering in larger amounts? Does your client need a product or service upgrade? Look at the total organization—are there other branches or departments that could use your product or service? Is the company opening any new branches, stores, or plants in the future? Are there sister companies that might be interested? In a person-to-person sale, are there other family members or friends who can also benefit from your expertise?

Follow Up on Referrals

If your customer is happy and successful with your product or service, he will generally be willing to help you make connections with others he knows. Ask for his help and then follow-up with the referrals immediately. And, if you do make other sales, make sure you thank your customer and give him some indication of your appreciation. While these gifts don't have to be expensive, they should be thoughtful and appropriate. Flowers and candy are generally safe, but if you know that your customer is a golf enthusiast, a new golf video might make a bigger hit. An invitation to your company's annual golf tournament might be even more impressive.

Intra-company referrals are just like gold. Your customer knows his organization and your product... if he tells you that another department or branch can use your product or service, you have an excellent chance of making a sale. And, because you've been referred by someone within the company, it's like you're family. You have already gotten over the hurdles of fear and distrust.

It's amazing how much gold salespeople leave lying around by not asking for referrals or thinking about account penetration. Every time they neglect an opportunity to ask for referrals, they're taking money out of their pocket and throwing it away. Every satisfied customer should be asked for referrals within and outside his family and organization. Remember the 1-5-15-30 strategy? As soon as you are confident that the customer's expectations are being met or exceeded, you should start looking for referrals.

The best time to ask for referrals is whenever you get positive feedback from the customer. For example, if a customer has just told you that he was able to produce a marketing brochure in less than a day using his new color copier, you could ask him if he knows anyone else who might want to be able to produce marketing materials that efficiently. By being specific about the benefit mentioned, you help focus your customer. It's a lot more powerful than just asking him if he knows anyone else who might like to have a color copier.

It also helps to get very specific about the source of the referrals. For instance, you might say, "That's great to be able to pull a marketing brochure together that quickly. Do you know anyone else in your local advertising association who might need to develop marketing materials that efficiently?" By being specific about the benefit and the source of the referrals, you'll allow your customer to go through his mental list of association members and pull out the names of people who might be interested.

But, it's important to get more than a name. Find out what makes your customer think the prospect might be interested—what has the referral said to indicate a need? What kind of business is he in? What type of person is the referral? What does he like or dislike? Find out as much as possible about the referral. This should be done in a casual way, of course. Your customer shouldn't be made to feel that he is revealing confidential information. Be sure to ask permission to use his name when you speak to his referral. If appropriate, ask him if he would be willing to call his associate and set up the appointment for you. If he agrees, it will significantly improve your chances for success.

Contact his referral as soon as possible. And, let your customer know the outcome of the contact. If the prospect winds up buying from you, be sure to acknowledge your customer appropriately. If the prospect doesn't buy, you should still send your customer a thank you note for the referral.

Review Your Customer's Buying Profiles

Always be thinking about how you can leverage your successes. Take advantage of every opportunity. You've worked hard to build and maintain your client relationship—don't be afraid to use it to get into places where you would not be able to otherwise, but be sure not to take advantage of your customers. Leverage includes asking for referrals, but it goes even further. You can further leverage your sales by studying the demographic and psychographic profiles of your present customers to lead you to new prospects who may have similar needs. This leads us full circle back to the Targeting step of the sales process!

Which is exactly right—it's a cycle. Each time you make a sale, look at the customer's profile. Analyze their situation and buying criteria. Look at their stage of development, decision-making process, and who's using which product for which applications. Determine the critical decision points in the sales process with this customer. Then look for other customers that might have similar needs, add them to your list of potential customers, and start contacting them.

Using your customer's profile to target other prospects is excellent, but leveraging doesn't stop there. You'll want to get a testimonial letter or a reference you can use to influence other potential buyers. Any happy customer is an excellent source for a testimonial letter. The best time to ask for one is when they compliment you on what a great job you're doing.

Customers are often willing to give you a letter, but sometimes they'll tell you they don't know how to write one. Tell them it would be helpful if they would answer these three questions: No.1: What factors were involved in your decision to buy from me rather than someone else? No.2: How has my product or service helped you? and No.3: Would you recommend me to others?

Testimonial letters are evidence of goodwill and they should be treated as an asset. Photocopy the originals and use them in bids, reports of findings and in your direct mail book. Obviously, you'll need to get permission first from your customer to use her testimonial letter in this fashion.

You want to make sure you talk to the customer so she knows how often her name might be used and how frequently she might be called upon to discuss your product or service. And, of course, you have to make sure that your customer is always satisfied and happy since potential customers will be calling her.

Summing Up

Your investment in creating a customer who will be your partner will pay off handsomely because he will make it easier for you to sell your next customer. Referrals make it easier because they help break the ice and remove some of the fear and distrust. Testimonials and references make it easier because they reduce the risk involved in the buying process. Substantial leverage is possible when you develop the right relationship with your customers.

If you make assuring customer satisfaction a regular part of your sales routine and develop a large, loyal customer base, you will, in effect, be investing in your future the way people invest in life insurance. Think of each customer as an annuity. In the beginning, you establish the relationship. This is like taking out the policy. Over time, you service and maintain the customer, always making sure he or she is satisfied. This is analogous to paying your insurance premiums. As your sales career progresses, you'll find that you'll have many customers who will give you lots of business. You might consider this the annuity stage, in which your previous investment is paying off.

We use this analogy to give you a long-term view of your sales career and the relationships you'll develop within it. Of course, there's no guarantee that every customer will provide you with income as a low maintenance annuity would, but each customer you cultivate adds to your income, your referral base and your reputation as a leader in your field.

WRAP UP

PUTTING IT ALL TOGETHER

▼

We hope you feel that we've lived up to our commitment to you to deliver a new kind of sales training book based on collaboration and partnering with your clients to create a long-term relationships. And we hope you've understood that what we've been talking about is not simply some new technique or a new set of sales words. What we're describing is a fundamental shift in the way you perceive your customer and in the way your customer perceives you. And it all begins with how you perceive yourself. You're changing jobs. You're changing from a person who "sells" things to a person who "consults" and "solves problems" with people to further their businesses or their lives.

In order to really benefit from this book, you not only need to change your behavior Vis a Vis your customer, you need to change your perception of yourself in the sales situation. The first thing you'll need to do is accept the challenge and believe that the Competitive Advantage principles work. They do work and soon you'll be putting them to work for yourself. You'll need to develop a plan for how you're going to incorporate these changes into your daily sales routine. Change your habits gradually. If many of the ideas you've heard here are new to you, begin using some of the simpler ones with your existing customers.

If you're already doing a lot of the things we've mentioned— congratulations! We hope you picked up a few ideas that will enable you to have even more success. But let's assume that this approach is somewhat different from the way you've been dealing with your prospective clients.

As we review the principles of The Competitive Advantage, select one imaginary client—one you would like to have become a lifelong customer by using these concepts.

We began with Targeting. The most important aspect of Targeting is composing your Competitive Advantage statement. Do you have it ready?

Can you quickly state your name, your company, a statement about a problem in your market and how you and your product or service solve that problem? Can you state what your competitive uniqueness and advantages are, in thirty seconds or less? If you can't, that's where you'll need to start.

Next you'll target your potential customers by identifying your best current customers. When you've chosen those you consider best, you look for three things: who bought what?... how EXACTLY did you find and sell to those customers?... and why did they buy what they bought? Having the answers to those questions points the way to where you'll find more customers who fit your "best customer" profile. You'll reach these new prospective customers in a variety of ways: personal advertising, sales promotions, and public relations such as publishing a newsletter or becoming a guest speaker. Or you can generate excellent publicity for yourself by writing in an established magazine or newsletter.

After Targeting comes Contacting. Again, because you want to establish a long-term relationship with this new client, you won't use hit and miss tactics. Or a big scattershot approach. You'll send one letter, then another, then a third. You'll call three to five days after you know the third letter should have arrived. Our guidelines here were: Mail to 4 new prospects everyday. Make it look personal and lumpy! Always include a headline and a P.S. Always include a reply card and a toll free number. Computerize your system and USE IT EVERYDAY.

You'll also use the telephone everyday to contact prospects and customers and in-person cold calls when they're appropriate. You might go back and review the section on how to handle pre-appointment objections at this point. The most important thing to remember about using any of these contacting approaches is to be prepared. Do your homework. Know your prospective customer's industry and as much about their current situation as you can. Remember, you're not selling a product or service; you're collaborating with your customer to solve a problem or create an opportunity with what you're selling.

Once you get an appointment and meet your prospective lifelong customer, you'll determine what their behavioral style is so you can approach them in a way that's comfortable for them. Review the section on Dominant Directors, Cautious Thinkers, Interacting Socializers and Steady Relaters. That will help you to identify whether people want a direct or indirect approach from you and whether they want you to be controlling or supporting in your discussion.

The nest stage—Exploring—is where you'll get a chance to get deeply involved with your prospect to determine exactly how your product or service can be of help. It's where the partnering process really begins. You've already done as much homework as you can about this company and its industry in general. Now you'll find out what their specific situation is.

The key to exploring is simple—ASK OPEN ENDED, VALUES DRIVEN, EXPLORING QUESTIONS. There are two reasons for this. One, you'll want to involve the customer in the whole process. And two, you'll want to find out as much information as you can in order to provide an analysis for him of his situation. You'll be looking for information on his current situation, his desired situation and any relevant past experiences that will affect his decision-making.

You'll also want to find out who the actual decision-makers are going to be when the time comes to purchase. You will establish success criteria. And you'll use the success criteria in the Assuring stage when you're checking back to see if the solution is really working.

A key skill you'll need to develop in the exploring stage is active listening. If you need help here, please review the section on listening.

After the Exploring stage you'll write a report of findings. It offers a menu of solutions with various options. The Collaborating stage begins when you and your prospective customer look together at the options you've created. When you're working with your client to select options and create a solution you'll keep the client as involved in the process as you are by regularly asking for feedback on the options presented. You'll also differentiate between a feature that's built into your product and a benefit that will make a difference to your client.

You'll then confirm the sale because you've followed the collaborative approach we've laid out in The Competitive Advantage. Getting a yes for a purchase means you'll move into implementing the solution for your client. If you were to get an unqualified NO at this point, you would maintain the relationship and ask if you might contact her again in three to six months or when appropriate. You've learned many techniques to help you discover why a customer might be raising a particular concern and how to address it in the context of a collaborative relationship. We talked about Price, Priorities, Politics, Personality or Postponement as temporary obstacles.

You've targeted your customer, contacted her, explored her needs with her, collaborated in developing solutions, confirmed her expectations or handled her concerns, and now she's become a one-time buyer. How will you create a lifelong customer? Through the final step—assuring. You'll need to make sure her success criteria are being met. Remember our 1-5-15-30 system for recontacting the customer. You'll send a short note the day you make the sale. You'll call 5 days after delivery to make sure it's been received and that there aren't any initial problems. Fifteen days later you'll call to ensure that everything is on track. Thirty days after the sale you'll send a small but meaningful gift. And then you'll have an annual review... more often if necessary, to make sure everything is meeting or exceeding the customer's expectations. You'll revisit the exploring stage to see what has changed and what new problems have arisen that you could address.

Building a Lifelong Quality Relationship with Your Customers

Your client has now become a source for possible referrals and the cycle begins again for you. Targeting, Contacting, Exploring, Collaborating, Confirming and Assuring. That cycle, or circle, is one of the major differences between what we've been calling traditional selling and what we're offering you here in this book.

In the past, sales was so often a one shot event... sell a product or service and go on to another prospect. Our approach will not only change your style of selling, it will change your life. One of the most common complaints from people in the world of business today is that we don't have enough time for quality relationships. That's a fringe benefit for you as you change your approach. You'll find that you'll develop many new friends along the way.

As you integrate our approach into your selling style, you may find that it feels awkward at first, because it's different from the way you've been selling. As you keep practicing, you'll soon begin to notice that the new way is more comfortable than the old way for you and your customers. Before long, you'll find that the collaborative approach will seem natural to you and you'll begin to for get the way you used to sell.

As you work the system, the system will work for you. Your constant attention to your customer's needs will help you to build your sales career and your competitive advantage.

Thanks for joining us in this sales training book. We wish you the best of luck and success in your career. Actually, you won't need luck you'll just need persistence. By working the collaborative selling system we've presented in this book, you'll create all the success you'll ever need, because you'll have The Competitive Advantage.

ABOUT THE AUTHORS
RICK BARRERA

▼

After an award winning sales career that included telemarketing, door-to-door, wholesale, retail, and business-to-business selling for both product and service based businesses, Rick Barrera launched Rick Barrera and Associates, Inc. to teach others his unique, highly effective, customer friendly sales methodologies. His client list includes Abbott Labs, Intel, Lexus, JD Edwards, Harley-Davidson, General Electric, Hewlett Packard and Washington Mutual.

He is co-author of "Non-Manipulative Selling," published by Prentice Hall Press and "The Dollars and Sense of Exceptional Service Delivery." Rick's latest book "Overpromise and Overdeliver: Using TouchPoint Branding to Design and Deliver Extraordinary Customer Experiences" made both the Wall Street Journal and Business week best seller lists. Overpromise and Overdeliver has just been released in Russian and Chinese.

He lives in San Diego with his wife and 2 sons.

He can be reached at Rick.Barrera@Barrera.com or (800) 835-4458.

Websites: www.overpromise.com and www.barrera.com

ABOUT THE AUTHORS
ANTHONY J. ALESSANDRA, PH.D.

Dr. Tony Alessandra helps companies build customers, relationships, and the bottom line. Companies learn how to achieve market dominance through specific strategies designed to outmarket, outsell, and outservice the competition.

Dr. Alessandra has a street-wise, college-smart perspective on business, having fought his way out of NYC to eventually realize success as a graduate professor of marketing, entrepreneur, business author, and keynote speaker. He earned his BBA from the University of Notre Dame, an MBA from the University of Connecticut and PhD in Marketing from Georgia State University.

Dr. Alessandra is founder and president of AssessmentBusiness-Center.com, president of Online Assessments, a company that offers online multi-rater assessments and tests; co-founder of MentorU.com, an online e-learning company; and Chairman of the Board of BrainX, a company that offers online digital accelerated-learning programs.

Dr. Alessandra is a widely published author with 14 books translated into 17 foreign languages, including Charisma (Warner Books, 1998); The Platinum Rule (Warner Books, 1996); Collaborative Selling (John Wiley & Sons, 1993); and Communicating at Work (Fireside/Simon & Schuster, 1993). He is featured in over 50 audio/video programs and films, including Relationship Strategies (American Media); The Dynamics of Effective Listening (Nightingale-Conant); and Non-Manipulative Selling (Walt Disney).

Recognized by Meetings & Conventions Magazine as "one of America's most electrifying speakers," Dr. Alessandra was inducted into the Speakers Hall of Fame in 1985, and is a member of the Speakers Roundtable, a group of 20 of the world's top professional speakers. Tony's polished style, powerful message, and proven ability as a consummate business strategist consistently earns rave reviews.

Contact: Dr. Tony Alessandra, Alessandra & Associates. Inc., 5927 Balfour Court, Suite 103, Carlsbad, CA 92008 Phone: 1-800-222-4383 or 1-702-567-9965 Fax: 1-760-603-8010 email: TA@Alessandra.com Website: www.Alessandra.com <http://www.Alessandra.com>

FREE BONUS OFFER
THE EDGE—6 HOUR AUDIO PROGRAM ON MP3S

▼

"Six easy Steps help you increase your sales, get more referrals, and earn higher commissions."

We spent years (and many, many thousands of dollars) putting together an easy to learn sales system that not only allows your customers to feel great about doing business with you, but they love to talk about the experience with their friends, who they send to you as well. It makes your job so much easier. When people come to you, the dynamics of selling change. You now have The Edge!

The Edge is built around our selling system called *Collaborative Selling*. It contains strategies and techniques that ensure you team up with your prospects. They now see you, not as a pesky sales person out to make a buck but, as an expert consultant working on their behalf.

Once you finish this audio program, you'll know each *Collaborative Selling* sales step and how and when to use them. This is not brain surgery—but it is powerful. It becomes second nature to you. You'll be able to watch as both your sales and your commissions smash your old records and set new standards.

Here is what you'll learn:
TARGETING YOUR TOP 20%

- How to find customers who want what you have and can afford it
- How to properly analyze where your most profitable business comes from
- How to get customers to think of you first when they are ready to buy
- Get people calling you instead of you calling them so you gain a competitive advantage in whatever you are selling

CONTACTING PROSPECTS

Master our direct mail campaign (don't worry, this is a small manageable way to use letters to keep you flooded with hot buyers. It works!)
- Learn how to write letters that sizzle with emotion to get your prospects to respond now

- Learn how people read letters so you can make your letters more powerful Learn two "no-cost" things you must always include to get a higher response from your direct mail pieces
- Learn how to overcome initial objections without coming across as pushy

EXPLORING NEEDS

- Learn our six-step process to becoming a much better listener
- Learn how to ask powerfully effective questions
- Discover the eight most important question topic areas and how to use each to uncover customer needs

COLLABORATING SOLUTIONS

- Learn how to determine your true competitive advantages so you get "one up" on your competition
- Discover how to get your prospect involved in coming up with their own solutions
- Learn the four key steps in creating options for your customer
- Learn how to ask effective feedback questions

CONFIRMING THE SALE

- Learn how to get your prospects to buy from you, instead of you having to sell them
- Learn how to recognize positive buying signals from your prospect

ASSURING CUSTOMER LOYALTY

- Learn our simple but very powerful four-step follow up system that will have your customers raving about you and sending you more business
- Learn how to plan a formal, annual review with your customers
- Learn how to leverage existing customers to expand your customer base

The Edge is a six hour audio program that will help you by keeping what you learn close at hand for study or to listen to as you need it. If it feels right to you and you're ready to make a drastic improvement in your sales results, get The Edge now.

For a FREE download of this bonus go to:
http://www.Alessandra.com/theedge

Claim Your Bonus: PeopleSmart Six Hour Audio Program on Downloadable MP3s

▼

Imagine...

- When you encounter difficult people—you know how to adapt to them.
- Where you meet challenging situations—you have the skills transform them.
- In times when you face the unknown—you remain fearless.

Imagine having a instantly downloadable product that will teach you to master the above skills that you can burn to a CD, put on your MP3 player, or access on your laptop or PC...

If you dream of all of that and more... Then PeopleSmart is the MP3 series you need. is a unique blend of scientific research on human behavior and my 30-plus years of teaching people smarts—through the Platinum Rule.

The PeopleSmart MP3 series is a unique blend of scientific research on human behavior and my 30-plus years of teaching people smarts using the Platinum Rule.

Once you've been exposed to these hands-on, proven and practical principles, you'll find that you will have access to uncommon wisdom allowing you to:

- Become a more loved and effective boss
- Gain effortless cooperation of even the most difficult people
- Fascinate and influence your spouse and children
- Build quick rapport that creates life long relationships
- Get along with all types of people from every walk of life

Curious about how PeopleSmart achieves all this?

Well, here's its secret formula...

Ever wondered why your natural behavior sometimes seems to alienate people?

It is because that same behavior may not be natural for others. You know in your heart—you have the highest intentions. If you want to get along with your colleagues, employees, bosses, friends, and family, it's essential to become aware of your natural tendencies—and their natural preferences!

Here is the key...

You must learn to determine and distinguish the four major behavioral styles.

PeopleSmart shows you how do this, by helping you to learn about your own style first, then showing you quick and easy ways to identify the styles of others. Finally, you learn how to adjust your behavior so that you become versatile, adaptable and widely popular.

It gets even better.

Learn to apply PeopleSmart and soon you unconsciously begin to draw out the best in everyone around you. You notice how easy it becomes for you to gain the trust and respect of even the most cynical people you meet.

The PeopleSmart MP3 series is very enjoyable to listen to and simple to apply.

Download yours today at www.Alessandra.com/peoplesmart

Here is just a fraction of what I cover in these six power-packed MP3s:

- How to treat others the way they want to be treated, not the way you want to be treated—without being phony or underhanded.
- A description of each behavioral style to help you determine which one you are.
- How to identify other people's styles.
- How to get along with everyone at work, school, home—anyone and anywhere.

This is a listener-friendly MP3 series. You can use and reuse it as a constant companion to consult when dealing with difficult people and stressful situations.

PeopleSmart gives you the tools to get what you want in various personal and work situations and equips you with the power and knowledge to cash in on these insights through more positive and productive exchanges with others.

You can realistically take charge of improving all your work relationships and this MP3 series tells you how.

ADDITIONAL LEARNING TOOLS
DISCstyles

An indisputable fact is that people prefer to interact with people they like. The ability to create rapport with people is a fundamental skill in sales, management, personal relationships, and everyday life. The goal of DISCstyles is to create personal chemistry and productive relationships. You do not have to change your personality. You simply have to understand what drives people and recognize your options for effectively dealing with them.

DISCstyles teaches you powerful life-skills that will serve you well in all your relationships: business, social and family.

To fully experience the magic of DISCstyles, take your DISCstyles Assessment now. http://www.DISCself.com/?mj

Dynamics of Effective Listening
Six Hour Audio Program on downloadable MP3s

Active Listening Skills: What they didn't teach you in school could be the key to becoming closer to your friends and family; a better, stronger leader; and finally able to explode your earning potential.

Active listening is a skill so important that anyone who lacks it is sure to have problems at home and at work: problems with a spouse, kids, customers, a boss (or bosses), or co-workers. When you don't know how to listen to others, you can't help but create misunderstandings that end up costing a lot of time and money. But those trends do not have to continue.

The Dynamics of Effective Listening is an MP3 audio program that will teach you how to effectively listen to others. Dr. Tony Alessandra and his thirty plus years of researching human behavior will help you tap into your own communication power. You can master the skill of active listening in just a few short weeks.

Buy It Now!
http://www.alessandra.com/products/productdetails.asp?productid=77

Astounding Customer Service
80-minute Audio Program on downloadable MP3s

Download this 80-minute MP3 series right now and you're moments away from acquiring the most critical and valuable skill that could mean thousands (maybe more) to your bottom-line.

How much is a valued customer really worth to your business? Do the math. It costs you up to 4 times more to get a new customer than it does to retain an existing one.

But wait...

That doesn't even take into account the fact that an unhappy customer will tell an average of 20 customers about their bad experiences, while a satisfied customer will only tell 10 people about their good experiences.

This means you have to make twice as many customers happy as unhappy—just to break even!

Call me stupid but I'm keeping my customers happy and satisfied... and the only way to do it is through Astounding Customer Service!

Download this 80-minute MP3 series right now on your computer and you're moments away from acquiring the most critical and valuable skill that could mean thousands (maybe more) to your bottom-line.

I've laid it all out for you here—over 35 years of the customer service secrets that have helped me tremendously in my own business career and saved me from many ruined customer relationships along the way.

Buy It Now!

http://www.alessandra.com/products/productdetails.asp?productid=78

How to Gain Power and Influence with People
5 1/2 Hour Audio Program on downloadable MP3s

When You Have This, You Never Have to Ask Twice!

Ever meet someone who made you feel small in his or her presence? Like they could see right through you, size you up, and get you to do pretty much anything they wanted?

It's a very strange feeling, believe me. You feel like you're being pulled in by a tractor beam. You desperately want to resist and despise this person. It could be a salesperson, your boss, even a relative. But you can't because they are just so darn charming and persuasive.

What's the big secret?

Well, as an applied behavioral scientist and human relationships expert, I have spent my entire career studying this mysterious effect and what I learned really surprised me...

There's no secret! What we commonly think of as the mystical, magical power of persuasion and influence is really just a set of practiced techniques any eleven-year old could follow.

In fact, if you had an hour today you could learn these cut and dry techniques for yourself and use them immediately on the people in your life to get them following immediately in line with your agenda!

Here's how to do that:

My research revealed some specific qualities that all powerful and influential people demonstrate. I used this research to create a system to help you and people like you strengthen their Power and Influence muscles.

The system is called How to Gain Power and Influence WITH People MP3 audio album.

And you can download it instantly!

This is 5 1/2 hours of pure fascination. Listen to it for just an hour and you will gain Power and Influence that will help you:

- Get far more respect than the average person does
- Be admired and adored, seemingly without effort
- Exude huge amounts of self-confidence and self-esteem
- Appear extremely powerful without being intimidating
- Easily get what you want, because people instinctively want to help you

With this system you get 12 Power and Influence-building sessions, covering:

Session 1   The Power of Charisma

Session 2   Maximizing Your Personal Power

Session 3   Making a Powerful First Impression

Session 4   Power Energy and the Aura of Success

Session 5   The Power of Because

Session 6   The Power of Space and Time

Session 7   Power Speaking

Session 8   Power Listening

Session 9   The Power of Personality

Session 10 Power Rapport

Session 11 Power Adaptability

Session 12 Testing Your Power and Influence

Buy It Now!

http://www.alessandra.com/products/productdetails.asp?productid=79

Mastering Your Message
5 Hour Audio Program on downloadable MP3s

Learn to communicate like a Boardroom Warrior!
* Do you ever feel like half the room is asleep during your presentations?
* Do you worry that your company meetings aren't productive—that people are leaving more unclear about things than when they came in?
* Are you frustrated with being overlooked, of not having an impact, of having a great idea but not knowing how to voice it?
* Are you self-conscious of the way you stand and speak—are you concerned that your body language may be sabotaging your career?
* When employee conflicts erupt, do you resolve them quickly, or do you add fuel to the fire by being tentative and non-direct?

This program will help you take your first steps on the path to becoming a masterful communicator, a wizard of interpersonal exchange, a Boardroom Warrior. Order my mp3, Mastering Your Message today, and experience for yourself the increase in personal power I am promising. You can download the entire program in less than 2 minutes by clicking on the link below. Within 45 minutes of listening to the very first volume, you'll be able to walk into work tomorrow like a changed person. (Your office will see it too!)

Buy It Now!
http://www.alessandra.com/products/productdetails.asp?productid=80

Simplicity—Five Hour Audio Program on downloadable MP3s

Lead a Happy, Balanced Life with Jeff Davidson and Tony Alessandra's "Simplicity" 12—Chapter MP3 Set:

Your sanity may depend on it!

When you are finally able to implement Simplicity in your life, that is, cut out the complexities that swallow your time and raise your stress level, you will notice that you'll have more time and energy to dedicate to strengthening the bonds with those that matter most. Stop juggling and learn how to live a happy, healthy, productive, stress-free, and well-balanced life. That's right, it's as simple as that. Now you can learn how to have it all too!

Buy It Now!
http://www.alessandra.com/products/productdetails.asp?productid=81

Alessandra on The Power of Listening downloadable MP3

Sharpen Your "Business Radar" In Just 60 Minutes!

- Do you forget important information the second you leave a meeting with a client, co-worker, or boss?
- Do you have a difficult time really focusing in on what the other person is saying without letting your own thoughts and pre-judgments get in the way?
- Are you missing out on the "silent messages" people are sending you through body language and gestures?
- Would you like to give yourself an edge in negotiations, picking up on the "subtle" clues of conflict and frustration other people miss?

Then unleash the Power of Listening!

Of all the business skills critical to your career and personal success, I rank powerful listening skills to be #1. Why? It's simple.

In case you haven't noticed, business today is about one thing: gathering information. The person who gathers the most "correct" information in the shortest period of time is most likely to make the correct judgments and the correct decisions. This is true for any position—from corporate executives to customer service!

If you're dealing with "cold" computer printouts and fact sheets all day, that's one thing. But if your job involves "warm" daily interaction with clients, customers, coworkers, and managers, then you know your primary tools for gathering this vital information will be your ability to "tune out" your own thoughts and distractions and completely "tune into" what the other person is saying. Both through their words and their body language.

But are your tools sharp enough?

Unfortunately, most of us are pretty lousy listeners. In your average conservation, you're lucky if you can process and retain 10% of what the other person is saying. This has nothing to do with memory and everything to do with how skilled you are at organizing and compartmentalizing information in your brain as soon as it comes in.

Thankfully for you, I've created The Power of Listening. This is an entertaining and informative MP3 audio program you can download right now that teaches you all the vital tricks to increasing your listening abilities so you can learn more, observe more, and retain more from each and every one of your conversations.

Having this information at your fingertips is like having a hand-held high frequency radar you can pull out during meetings, client presentations, and everyday office interactions so that no vital information slips through the cracks. Not only can you process and remember more of what anyone says, but you'll be able to tell if what they're saying is actually the truth! Do their words match their actions? Is someone nervous, or are they open and calm? The Power of Listening teaches you!

Buy It Now!

http://www.alessandra.com/products/productdetails.asp?productid=85

Alessandra on NonVerbal Communication—downloadable MP3
Be the Master of Your Unspoken Message

Have you ever allowed your eyelids to droop at a conference, made jarring hand motions in a boardroom meeting, delivered a podium address with weak vocal intonation... and not even been aware of it? Did you know that what you don't say can have a great affect on how everyone perceives you?

Likewise, do you know what to look for in others' nonverbal messages?

For example, an employee enters your office, shoulders slouched, body rigid, and sits down with his arms and legs crossed. His lips perched and fists clenched, he avoids all eye contact and makes nervous, fidgeting gestures.

You give him the benefit of the doubt and believe what he says. However, if you knew the secrets of NonVerbal Communication, you could have read his body language and exposed him for lying.

Know for sure by learning the language of NonVerbal Communication!

The way you communicate nonverbally is responsible for 90 percent of what people think of you. It's the difference between being considered weak or powerful, unsure or confident, insecure or ready to take on the world. You could use authoritative words, have excellent listening skills, or be an expert with feedback, but if you don't understand nonverbal communication, your communication and ability to detect what others are communicating is not as effective as it should be.

Knowing exactly what to look for in your own gestures and vocal intonations will help you communicate a powerful message, confidence, and an assured presence. On the flip side, having a keen eye for others' unspoken messages will enable you to know what they are really saying—before they open their mouths to speak.

Alessandra On NonVerbal Communication MP3 will help you get it right!

In just the one hour it takes to listen to my Alessandra On NonVerbal Communication MP3, you'll walk away knowing how to target yours and others' specific gestures, movements, vocal intonations—and decipher what they all mean. It really works. Once you understand this non-verbal language, you'll be able to use it to your advantage. The winner in you will consistently shine through, and no one will be able to fool you again.

Buy It Now!

http://www.alessandra.com/products/productdetails.asp?productid=86

The Platinum Rule—Two-Hour DVD

Dr. Tony Alessandra delivers a LIVE program in front of several hundred business people in a Detroit theatre. You get nearly 75 dynamic minutes of The Platinum Rule topic and a BONUS of nearly 45 minutes on Customer Loyalty and Collaborative Selling on a single DVD. Lucky for you and me, there were two studio-quality cameras rolling that caught every word, every laugh, and every nugget-of-wisdom Tony had to share that day. Now you can laugh as you learn how to gain instant rapport and get along with nearly anybody you meet no matter who they are.

That day, Dr. Tony Alessandra, author of 13 books, veteran of over 2,000 paid speeches, taught several hundred people the easiest, most fun way to master people skills and selling skills. Now he wants to teach you too.

Yes. There have been countless books and videos produced on this subject, but if you weren't in Detroit, you have not seen the best of the best. And it was magic.

"If you have ever had a personality conflict with another human being—get this DVD."

After you watch this DVD, you'll understand why corporations like IBM, Ford, AT&T and numerous other Fortune 500 companies are willing to pay Tony thousands of dollars for 60 minutes of his time.

But don't be fooled. Even though Tony keeps you laughing, he doesn't forget to deliver powerful content. Apply the simple techniques Tony shares with you and you get immediate results.

Dr. Tony has spent over 30 years tweaking his findings into two simple questions. Know the answers to these two questions, along with some additional knowledge Tony shares with in this highly entertaining DVD, and you hold the key to one of the most powerful human relationship concepts in the world. Don't put off getting this DVD of Dr. Tony in action. You'll watch it again and again.

Buy It Now!

http://www.alessandra.com/products/productdetails.asp?productid=23

The Platinum Rule Video Training

How to train your team to have instant rapport and immediate chemistry with your customers, suppliers and each other.

"Whether you're selling, negotiating, or dealing
with problem customers, knowing and applying
The Platinum Rule will increase your success."

Your people will get interested right from the start. Unlike many training films done in studio with "talking-heads"—this was filmed in front of a "live" audience of hundreds of people. Dr. Tony Alessandra shares his simple, fun and easy to understand techniques on how to deal with other people much more effectively.

It's fun. It's easy. It works!

Yes. There have been countless books, and videos produced on this subject—but if you haven't seen Dr. Tony, you have missed the best of the best. Tony's "from-the-streets-of-New York City style" is anything but boring. It's pure magic. But best of all, it's filled with immediately usable and effective content.

"If your employees have ever had a personality conflict with one of your customers—get this video training series."

After your people experience this training—you'll understand why corporations like IBM, Ford, AT&T and numerous other Fortune 500 companies are willing to pay Tony thousands of dollars for only 60 minutes of his time.

This program is a comprehensive video-based training program that can be taught in either a half-day or full-day format. It includes a 48-minute video divided into several sections with lively lecturettes as well as entertaining vignettes by professional actors. It also includes a comprehensive 100+ page leader's guide with easy step-by-step instructions for facilitating the entire training program. Plus, it includes 10 extensive participant kits, each of which includes an invaluable assessment-package consisting of one self-evaluation, five observer evaluations, and a scoring matrix; a 63-page workbook, a 40-minute audio summary of the course, and a laminated pocket-sized summary card for reinforced learning.

But don't be fooled. Even though Tony keeps you laughing—he doesn't forget to deliver high caliber "customer-satisfying" content. It's simple. Apply the easy-to-understand and proven techniques Tony shares with you, and you get immediate results.

Buy It Now!
http://www.alessandra.com/products/productdetails.asp?productid=24

Flexibility eWorkbook—25-page PDF eWorkbook

Do you respond to certain people, conditions, or events out of fear or anxiety? Are you unwilling to change your perspectives or positions in certain situations? Do you tend to face ambiguous situations negatively? If so, you may have predetermined views, conclusions, or patterns of behavior that are driving your actions—and impairing your flexibility. When you voluntarily refrain from participating in certain situations or interacting with certain people because of your lack of flexibility—therefore limiting your horizons—you decrease your chances of personal and professional success.

The Flexibility eWorkbook is an interactive tool for analyzing your personal attitudes toward yourself, others, and the situations you face. This workbook is a powerful tool that will help you dispel those attitudes that are holding you back from realizing your full potential.

Topics covered include:

• Helping you increase your tolerance and respect for others, your confidence, and your positiveness—all of which enhance your flexibility

• Helping you decrease your rigidity, discontent, and competitive drive—all of which hinder your flexibility

Buy It Now!
http://www.alessandra.com/products/productdetails.asp?productid=61

Versatility eWorkbook—27-page PDF eWorkbook

Are you stuck in a rut? Do you maintain the same routine way of doing things, regardless of changes in circumstances? If so, you may lack versatility—and you may be suffering the consequences as change passes you by.

The Versatility eWorkbook is an interactive tool for helping you dispel attitudes of low versatility that may have become deeply ingrained as a part of your basic personality. This workbook will help you change some of your habitual behaviors and knee-jerk reactions in order to become